- How can I help my father keep his dignity despite his medical problems?

- What should I watch for when touring a nursing home?

- How are my parents' nutritional needs changing now that they're older?

- I sometimes lose my patience with my mother . . . how can I improve our relationship?

If you're caring for a parent, you probably have a lot of questions. *When Parents Age* is the book that offers answers . . . as well as tips, suggestions, and solutions for all the situations a caregiver faces.

Includes information on . . .

- HEALTH ISSUES
- CON GAMES: HOW TO PREVENT YOUR PARENTS FROM BEING CHEATED
- THE QUESTION OF PRIVACY
- HELPING PARENTS EXERCISE AND KEEP FIT
- HOW TO DEAL WITH A HARD-OF-HEARING PARENT
- HANDLING INSURANCE MATTERS

AND MORE

WHEN PARENTS AGE:
What Children Can Do

Tom Adams
and
Kathryn Armstrong

BERKLEY BOOKS, NEW YORK

WHEN PARENTS AGE: WHAT CHILDREN CAN DO

A Berkley Book / published by arrangement with
the authors

PRINTING HISTORY
Berkley trade paperback edition / March 1993

ISBN: 0-425-13581-0

A BERKLEY BOOK ® ™ 757,375
Berkley Books are published by The Berkley Publishing Group,
200 Madison Avenue, New York, New York 10016.
The name "BERKLEY" and the "B" logo
are trademarks belonging to Berkley Publishing Corporation.

PRINTED IN THE UNITED STATES OF AMERICA

10   9   8   7   6   5   4   3   2   1

To our mothers,
Inez Berryhill Adams
and
Ruth Armstrong

ACKNOWLEDGMENTS

Many people gave information, guidance and support as we wrote this book about children helping their aging parents.

From the beginning, Elizabeth Beier, our editor at The Berkley Publishing Group, eagerly embraced the idea for this book.

George Greenfield of Lecture Literary Management encouraged us to develop this timely book. Through personal interviews with children and their aging parents, valuable insights and experiences were shared. We are indebted to the following: Ona and Bernice, Inez and Ruth, Ida and Kay, Louise and Gerard, and Bill.

In addition to the interviews, we were assisted by Howard and Marion Higman, Tom Eaton, Phillip Adams and Thomas Armstrong. Rosa Grundig and Stephanie O'Haver provided editorial and technical services.

Finally, we applaud the children who love and care for their aging parents and other relatives. Together, they enrich lives and leave a legacy for others to follow.

INTRODUCTION

"At our twentieth college reunion, we talked with pride about our children. At our thirtieth reunion, we talked with concern about our parents: How could we help them age with dignity?"

—Chloe Aaron, filmmaker

How can we help our parents age with dignity? More and more adult children are confronted with this challenge. While families once grew old together and most parents died before they reached a point of diminished capacities, today's situation is very different. Of those who have reached seventy, the current life expectancy is eighty-one and one-half years for men and eighty-six for women. Children now have to make many important decisions with their parents, often in the face of failing health and depleted resources. Because this condition is new, most children are unaware and unprepared for the emotional, financial, medical, and social challenge.

WHEN PARENTS AGE

When Parents Age: What Children Can Do explores this rapidly growing phenomenon and offers guidance and understanding to adult children as well as to other caregivers of the elderly.

Most parents are—and wish to—remain independent. As you read this book, accept one guiding principle: encourage your parents to remain in charge of their lives as long as they can and offer to assist them when and if they need you. Chances are they will do so at some point. Let them know that you are there and will abide by their decisions because you respect their wisdom and independence.

This book is based on the experiences of the authors and on interviews with other adults who live with and assist their aging parents. Issues are discussed, helpful hints are provided for each topic, and personal family anecdotes provide insights and instruction as well as inspiration and example. On top of the helpful hints, specific information directs the reader to agencies offering services to the elderly.

Chapter 1, When Parents Age, discusses aging—as it was in the past (since many of our parents are products of another era) and as it occurs today. The role of children as caregivers to their parents is examined, and emotional and social concerns are presented. Not all children can or should assume this often frustrating, demanding, and poignant task; the decision is for you and your parents to make this judgment call.

Aging in Place and Other Options, Chapter 2, explores one of the most important concerns: Where and how will parents live as they grow old and, possibly, become infirm? Living independently, in shared housing, in retirement communities, in board and care homes, in a reassembled family with their children, and, finally, in nursing homes are the options discussed here.

Chapter 3, Health Care—Primary Concerns, examines health promotion, prevention, chronic illness, and dying and death. No other issue elicits as much emotion and compassion as dealing with the health concerns of our parents. To watch them become increasingly vulnerable is traumatic. Things can be done to enhance their vitality.

Children can do many things to enrich and safeguard their parents' final years. Knowing how can bring joy to both. Chapter 4, Enriching the Final Years, provides simple, easy-to-accomplish examples of how aging can be a time of continued growth and mutual support.

Finally, knowledge of available resources is essential to both parents and children. In most communities, abundant public and private resources can be found. An annotated list, specific to aging in place, health concerns, legal and financial matters, and enrichment is provided in Chapter 5, Resources. Learn about these valuable programs and how to use them when appropriate.

In your childhood, you may have had the good fortune to be loved and taught by devoted parents. If so, your parents' aging presents you with the opportunity to return compassion. Use as much of this book's guidance as you can. As you read it, think about what you want to and can do. Throughout the book, brief stories based on actual experiences are presented in order to illustrate the points made by the authors.

He's My Memory Now

"Preston always asked me to will him my memory. He couldn't believe that I could remember things as far back as the 1890s. Well, he wouldn't want my memory now. I can't remember anything." She turned to her son and asked, *"Did I write to Gusta today? I can't remember."*

"Yes, you wrote a long letter this morning telling her about the patio and how much you like to sit among the flowers and feel the warm sun on your arms."

"I did? I can't remember when I wrote her. I do like to sit on the patio. I'm glad Rick fixed the fence so the dogs can't get in. When the days get warmer, I'll let you take me outside."

"Did you have a dog when you were young?"

"Oh, yes. I called him Spain. He was the cutest little fat white dog with brown spots. He'd go with me everywhere. They all knew I was coming down the road when they saw Spain. He ran ahead of me when I went to see Blanche Walker. She always knew I was coming because Spain beat me there every time. Then she'd see me walking down the road. We'd walk back and forth from her house to Grandmother Thomas's house where I stayed. We'd talk all the way. Spain liked to get out and run. He was the nicest little dog."

"I like that name—Spain. Why did you call him that?"

"Grandmother named him. He was her dog. Maybe she always wanted to travel to Spain."

"Who was Blanche Walker?"

"My best friend from the time I was twelve until I went away to school at sixteen."

Her son paused. "You have a wonderful memory. Preston will get a prize."

"Not anymore. I can remember the past, but I can't remember today. Now I do remember writing the letter this morning. It's a good thing you're here. You're my memory now."

Her son is her memory and much more, and she is the nurturer whose life spans a century. Inez and other parents continue to teach and inspire. Their stories evoke memories of the past as well as their struggle to adapt to aging in a society that has yet to come to grips with a human condition that will dominate much of the next century.

WHEN PARENTS AGE:
What Children Can Do

CHAPTER 1

————— ❖ —————

When Parents Age

Many adult children are never confronted with problems associated with aging because their parents live independently until death. And, of course, some lose their parents early in life and miss the joys and sorrows of seeing them grow old. A dream shared by parents and children alike is that they will age and die with dignity and independence. The older generation fears becoming a burden, facing failing health, being alone, and losing control. Together, children and parents can do many things to enrich each other's lives.

All too often, growing old is portrayed as negative and foreboding. According to a 1991 Gallup survey, the average American does not wish to live beyond eighty-five. In the face of a terminal illness or plagued with pain, many would prefer to depart immediately. They cannot bear the thought of requiring close attendance and care and the idea of their children having to shoulder the burden. Haunted by such fears, they can become bitter and hostile. Many resign themselves to their plight and live in solitude.

If, in the Western world, we were to learn from the primitive societies to revere the wisdom and spirituality that comes with age and to include our parents in an extended family—or even just from the way many families stayed together in the first part of the twentieth century—our parents would feel better about their place in society. They would see a role for themselves. Clearly, we have to stop assuming that the elderly will just fend for themselves. Clearly, we have to ensure that our aging parents fulfill a good life by becoming engaged in this pursuit. A nation that does not care about its elderly will lose its spirit.

You Learn to Save

The fire had been burning under the cauldron long enough to bring the well water to a boil. Virginia had carried the two large pails of well water to the spot near the house where they'd do the laundry in the yard.

"You learn to save," she told her daughter who'd helped sort out the clothes on the porch. "Water's hard to come by—like most other things out here on the prairies. Bernice, do you have them ready?"

"Yes, Momma."

"The water's boiling, so let's get on with it." Virginia took the stack of white clothes and put them in the soapy

2

water, moving them around with a long stick. Next, she took the stack of not-so-dirty clothes to follow the white ones. When they were done, she took the pile of colored clothes and gave them their turn in the boiling water. Finally, she took the stack of dirtiest clothes (those her husband wore on the oil rigs) and completed the washing.

After dumping the hot, dirty water onto the ground, they carried the wet clothing to a large zinc tub filled with cold water on the back porch and rinsed them in the same order used in the washing.

"Bernice, we're lucky it's warm weather. When snow comes, fires don't start so easy outside. You'll see." Virginia pushed the warm garments about in the tub of cold water to remove the soap. She rinsed each pile twice and, with her strong hands, she wrung the water from them onto the ground by the back porch.

"Can I take this load to hang out to dry?" Bernice asked. She had watched her mother wash each week for years.

"Fine. Hang them careful so as not to snag them on the barbwire." The fence served many purposes: It kept the cow in, kept out tumbleweed, held wet clothes, and discouraged would-be intruders. On dry, windy days, clothes didn't take too long. It was the wet, cold ones that made washing a long ordeal.

"Take that tub over there and put it by the porch to catch some rainwater. Then I'll be glad to wash your hair in it. It'll make it soft and curly," the mother instructed her daughter. She knew it was time to teach her the ways of the plains.

In the evening, Virginia hooked up her gas iron and

3

commenced her ironing. Out in those west Texas towns, women didn't have to heat the iron on a hot stove top. They used gas irons and felt privileged to cheat in this work.

Virginia learned to save on the prairie. She saved water, wood, jars, paper, string, nails, heat in a house, cloth material, cardboard, toys, and Christmas ornaments. Saving and handing down things went together.

Living Longer But Not Necessarily Better Lives

At the turn of the century, the average age was forty-seven; today it is seventy-five for men and seventy-nine for women. More than two million Americans are eighty-five or older, and this age group is increasing faster than any other. To have a living parent for a child of sixty-five is no longer unusual. As life expectancy increases, we must make longer lives better lives. If we don't, we are merely talking about survival in a disabled and dependent state.

In pre–World War II America, family life was shared, with the various members helping one another grow and age gracefully. Religious beliefs served as anchors to soften the hardships and guide daily life. The years following the Great War brought mixed blessings: freedoms, mobility, affluence. Dazzled by the newly found possibilities, some people lost their commitment to traditional values and became adrift. Religious institutions have ceased to have the stabilizing influence on people's lives, and our parents' heritage has been replaced by a popular culture controlled by mass media. The essential interdependence of work roles that once bonded families has largely disappeared, and many struggle to maintain mutual sharing. The only glue that holds some families together is made of compassion. Hopefully it will be strong enough to survive the pressures and stresses testing daily family life.

Caught in this immense social change are those whose age renders them vulnerable and often expendable. As our parents' circle of friends dwindles and the values they cherish are assaulted, we watch their quiet dismay.

Statistics leave no doubt that the prospects for a long and healthy life are grim for anybody who has either lived in poverty, has been abused, or is a member of an ethnic minority. These people's lives are shortened by malnutrition, early chronic illnesses, crime, poor medical care, and a host of other factors that place them on the sidelines of society.

They Are Our History

Think of what life was like for anyone over age seventy-five today. They were young during World War I, when life was often harsh, demanding, and full of sacrifices. Our parents lived during an era in which World Wars, the Great Depression, and magnificent technological and scientific advances tested them. Their small, intimate world grew rapidly as modern machines and conveniences replaced their self-reliance and hard work. They can only reflect on a time that has passed and will never reappear.

Self-Sufficient and Clannish

"Inez, if you marry that boy, you'll live by a creek and drink branch water the rest of your life," her father warned as he walked across the churchyard with his sixteen-year-old daughter. The year was 1906.

"But Papa, Fred's a nice boy," Inez protested lightheartedly. She was beautiful, popular, interested in several other boys anyway, and had no intentions toward marriage at that time. In a few days, she would leave McKenzie, west Tennessee, and enter college in Mississippi.

"He's a farm boy—lives way back in those hills, and you can do better than that."

As they strolled in the warm August sun, Walter Berryhill looked back at the white-frame Presbyterian church his father had helped build shortly after the end of the Civil War. The church was raised on four acres of farmland donated by his father, Stephen Jefferson Berryhill. It rested on large, two-feet-high limestone blocks, and grass grew beneath it. A family graveyard flanked one side under the shade of large oak trees, where well-tended gravestones traced the lines of Scot family members who had migrated from Mecklenburg County to inhabit "Little North Carolina," as this small enclave in the wooded and red clay fields of west Tennessee was affectionately called. The twenty Scot families farmed and traded, grew corn and cotton, raised livestock, married young, and bore children. On Sundays, they spent the day at their New Hope Presby-

terian Church. They were self-sufficient and clannish. Inez was different in several ways—she wanted a college education and fancied a life of travel. Her daddy said, "Travel alone is an education. Take any invitation you get to go places. I'll pay." She did. Inez's mother had died on June 10, 1891, during Inez's birth—from uremic poisoning—and Mammy, an aunt, had taken Inez to their nearby farm and raised her with her own five children. Inez was told about her mother when she was eight years old. She vowed then to give her life to her own children someday, and she would do just that, in many different ways.

The Sweet Child

Louise could take the train anywhere with her family because her daddy worked and died for the railroad. They'd go from Cowin to St. Louis, to Chattanooga, to Nashville, and make a day of it. Taking the Number Six to Chattanooga and spending the day on Signal Mountain was her favorite. The folks in her small town thought she was a special child because she traveled to places they only knew by name. She was the sweet child; that's what her grandmother, with whom she lived as a child, called her, because, as the oldest and gentlest, she was special. To be called "the sweet child" is an appellation of love. Louise lived in the church town, as the blacks said of those who were religious and refined. The others were said to live in the graveyard field because they were more likely to seek trouble and did not always follow the teachings of the church.

As a Methodist, Louise spend much of her childhood on church activities and attended Turner College in Shelby-

7

ville, Tennessee, where she studied to be a teacher. After graduation, Louise moved to Winchester to teach kindergarten.

Quiet, shy, and sheltered, Louise rarely challenged the dictates of the church elders. However, her independent nature landed her in trouble once when she traveled to Suwanee with some older friends and broke several church rules. She danced and enjoyed it. Word of this escapade traveled back home quickly, and Louise was summoned to appear before the church elders. Unrepentant, she was temporarily turned out of the church, only to be restored in due course, however.

Louise and Gerard met in Tampa, Florida, in 1925, and, following a brief courtship, Gerard told his mother, "We don't have to go to heaven to find an angel. I found her here in Tampa." They have been married for sixty-five years.

The Job's Played Out

Dear Daddy,
Momma's sick. We don't have any food to eat. We need you. Please come home.

Your loving son,
Junior

James Carroll read the letter at least a dozen times before he folded it and stuck it in the top pocket of his overalls. He walked to the basin, took the jug of coal oil from the shelf, and began to wash the oil and grime from his chapped hands. Dirt clung in the deep cracks in his skin, leaving

8

the traces of a string of oil fields across West Texas. He dried his hands with an old rag that hung by the basin.

Working in the oil fields was all he could find. The Depression sapped the jobs from the land the way the hot Texas sun wilted the shallow crops. James was not afraid to work. He could do anything any other man did on those rigs, winter or summer alike.

As he put the coal oil away, he knew what must be done. He'd go home. Besides, this job had played out. There had been no paycheck for a month. He reckoned things couldn't be any worse back in Van Zandt County. At least he could help Virginia and the kids. His heart ached to think about sickness and hunger moving all over God's creation.

"I'm better off than some," he whispered as he packed his few belongings in the old leather suitcase that accompanied him. "I'll hitch a ride into town."

James felt proud as he walked toward the office to tell the boss he'd be going home.

He wondered if Virginia knew that the oldest boy had written this plea for help. "Probably not," he thought. "That boy has gumption."

Who Gives Care When the Time Comes?

As parents reach and pass the age of sixty-five, children realize that both they and their parents' lives are changing. Already, many are taking responsibility for an aging relative by the time they are thirty, usually a widowed mother. The caregiving, most frequently, falls to one family member rather than the entire family. A healthy spouse may assist the other until this is no longer possible or required. Recent studies show that in three out of four cases, it is a daughter who assumes the caregiving tasks. With more than half of those daughters working outside the home and almost half of them still raising their own children, their lives become very full and demanding. Since women live longer than men, the parent cared for is most often the mother. These daughters often spend more years caring for a parent than for their own children. With most parents living into their eighties and nineties and with fewer children per family, nearly every woman will take care of an aging parent or parent-in-law at some time in her life.

Women who assume this complex and often exhausting additional role want others to realize that they need more understanding from their employers, more help and emotional support from the men in their lives, and better community services. Sons who care for a parent tend to shun community services and prefer paying for outsiders. Not traditionally holding nurturing roles, they also tend to shy from tasks such as dressing and bathing. However, they do provide emotional support most of the time, and the usual pattern is that sons offer financial help while daughters or daughters-in-law do the hands-on care.

Reflections on Aging

People age in unique ways and different stages: rapidly or gradually. They give up things once routine and accepted. By keeping a list of discontinued behaviors, you can understand your parent's aging process. This assessment can guide your response to health needs and, in particular, shed light on ways you may be able to enrich their lives as capacities diminish.

Inez's Chronicle

At age ninety-four, Inez began discarding old ways and daily things and, as she reached one hundred, her once-active life became quiet and simple.

1985: (age 94)	Makes her last summer trip to Tennessee to open the house to guests and family.
	Stops watering the garden.
	Uses a walking cane.
1987: (age 96)	Takes a sponge bath instead of a shower.
	Uses a magnifying glass to read books and newspapers. Cataracts develop.
	Uses a second walking cane for balance.

Receives the last letter from a close friend (all others deceased earlier).

1988:
(age 97)

Stops dusting and house cleaning.

Declines to go out to eat, shop, or ride in the car.

1989:
(age 98)

Uses a walker (after three falls).

Discontinues preparing the meals and having them in the kitchen.

Requires help with bathing and dressing.

Stops doing the laundry, but continues to fold her clothes, especially the pads she uses for incontinence.

Walks only from bedroom to living room and sits on the couch all day to watch television, look outside, and read.

Uses travel chair to get from bedroom to living room. Walks from couch to dining room for meals.

Stops going to beauty shop. Has hair cut at home by her favorite beautician.

Stops answering the telephone and taking messages.

Stops dialing telephone numbers.

Stops getting ready for bed alone.

Requires help with medication.

1990:
(age 99)

Stops reading letters.

Writes shorter letters to regular corre-spondents.

Requires help to change her pads for her incontinence. She must be assisted to stand while the pads are changed.

Loses short-term memory in some in-stances.

Stops eating chocolates and candy. These foods induce diarrhea.

1991:
(age 100)

Writes short letters.

Eats three prepared meals unassisted.

Reads the headlines of newspapers and magazines.
Uses an amplified telephone.

Walks assisted once a day to the dining room table.

Watches television.

Recognizes people by name and appear-ance.

Drinks weak, decaffeinated coffee and tea.

Carries on interesting conversations.

	Helps with her bath and dressing.
	Sits on the patio on warm days and enjoys the flowers and sunshine.
	Sits on the couch and watches the neighborhood.
	Remembers the past and tells engaging stories that describe the turn of the century and life during the past hundred years.
1991 (age 101)	Stops reading the headlines of newspapers and magazines.
	No longer walks; uses a travel chair.
	Continues all other activities of the previous year.

Most of Inez's changes occurred during the previous six years. She shows no sign of depression today. Keeping this chronicle helps her son understand her aging and plan enrichments.

You'll Make Your Mark

Sitting at the dining room table, Aunt Essie instructed Inez in manners and deportment as though she were preparing her own daughter to enter society. During her first few years at Mississippi Synodical College in Holly Springs, Inez boarded with Uncle Charles and Aunt Essie, her Presbyterian kin from west Tennessee. Uncle Charles was the pastor at the girl's school as well as for the town's main Southern Presbyterian church. Stern, yet humorous, he guided his young niece's spiritual and secular educa-

tion. As chairman of the Board of Trustees of the denominational college, he carefully followed Inez's education, while his wife looked after her niece's personal character.

"Well, Inez, what were your grades this month?" Uncle Charles inquired with appropriate concern. He wiped his mouth with a cloth napkin and placed the soup spoon in the Wedgwood bowl while awaiting Inez's reply.

"I did very well in science. I made a 98 in geology and a 95 in biology."

"That's good. Continue," he encouraged.

Inez paused as she moved the tall glass of water to the opposite side of the plate. "I made a 90 in English and 89-¾ in Latin."

"That's acceptable. Go on."

"A 75 in Theology," she whispered.

"Hmmm." The uncle took a long sip of cold water. He smiled and said, "Well, Inez, it's clear that you will make your mark on earth and not in heaven."

Soft laughter filled the room.

What Children as Caregivers Should Know

No easy answers are available to those who assume this responsibility. Most are unprepared for a complicated, often exhausting, and uncharted journey. Different situations present different challenges. For most, it is a task of balancing caring and employment, other family demands, and their own personal needs.

Begin today by sitting down with your parents and

discussing the future frankly. Include other significant family members. Say that you have concerns they most likely share and that you think talking about them before a crisis is useful. If your parents are receptive, speak honestly and directly to the issues this book examines.

Explore Feelings

In the discussion, frankly explore the options about where your parents will live, especially if they can no longer remain in their own residence. If they need help, you may not be the one to provide it because of some of the many factors that may make it impossible:

- Your own family needs are excessive.
- The distance between your homes is insurmountable.
- Past personal conflicts cannot be put aside and mutual trust is absent and unlikely to develop.
- Financial and occupational constraints make caring for your parents impossible.
- Parents and loved ones deny all need for such discussion.

However, you do need to discuss the situation and learn if there are things you can do, even in a limited way. The most painful feeling of all is estrangement from each other.

Some families are fraught with turmoil. Relationships

are hostile or unresolved, and entering a new, demanding one may be inappropriate. The caregiving may properly go to another family member or to paid helpers. Decide upon the best option, without guilt and rancor. Remember, each of you will change in the course of this experience. Your parents will age and may lose their original mastery of having been a parent to you. You will also change as new tasks are assumed. Be prepared to experience these changes. They are difficult to accept emotionally, especially as you witness loss of independence—theirs, as well as some of your own. Early planning with your parents can help you avoid a crisis—a crisis that could create unbearable stress and personal pain.

Choose This Role for Positive Reasons

Some children take care of their parents for the wrong reasons: they feel guilty, want to be a martyr, or want to control and punish their parents for past perceived wrongs. Aging makes your parents vulnerable and, in the final years, they may become only a shell of what they once were. To care for them when you don't want to or cannot do so without considerable stress is to invite trouble for all. Put all your feelings on the table. You may find that revealing your feelings assuages old angers and hurts. Consider rehearsing the conversation with a friend. Sometimes the sound of your own voice approaching these topics can help you organize your thoughts. Remember, your parents may need you just as you needed them as a child. If you do provide care for them, do it in a compassionate manner—openly, honestly, and realistically. Always be aware of how you feel about this new role. Do not hide your feelings. Honest anger and frustration are easier to accept than false pretenses and hidden rage. Watching them age as you give up parts of your life can make you angry and hurt. Accept that and go on to meet the challenges with as much warmth as you can muster.

Make Decisions Together

Shared decisions usually produce the best results, and your parents have the right to make their own decisions, even though you may not always agree. When decisions have to be made about a place to live, medical treatment, financial investments, or safety concerns, discuss the topics calmly and examine possible approaches. You may want to consider the views of a third party such as a minister, a good friend, a medical specialist, or others. Avoid making a decision that cannot be changed if conditions warrant. Also, consider why the particular decision is being made—for the parents' best interests or for your convenience. Do not make promises that you may not be able to keep, such as "We'll never put you in a nursing home." You may feel that way, but keep it a silent promise to yourself. Broken promises hurt.

Know Financial Constraints

At times, a decision may be dictated by financial limitations. Perhaps nursing home care is out of the question. Medicare does not cover long-term care, and Medicaid will pay for nursing homes and residential home care in some states but only after the aging parent has depleted most assets and lives at near poverty level. They may be faced with using their life savings, and you may find that family members must spend their own money to ensure proper care. In these cases, you need to consider what's best for you and your own family. Remember, most aging parents abhor becoming dependent and burdensome. Catastrophic and some chronic illnesses can be financially ruinous. Try to assess the health situation and plan appropriately. Family members can split costs as well as chores. The most important point for all is to feel in control as much as possible.

Face Good Times, Bad Times

Certainly, caregiving can bring great rewards and allow you to fulfill love and commitment to your parents. Those who approach the tasks with positive thoughts and compassion will enjoy the experience better than those who assume the role for wrong reasons. There will be good days and bad days, largely depending upon the health of your parents and their attitude toward aging. Even if they are in a nursing home, you can visit regularly and respond kindly to lonely phone calls. Being dependent and ill can create anger and resentment from both sides. Learn to set limits for yourself and enforce them. Explain why you are trying to bring things under control, but guard against treating them like children. If the time comes when you feel incapable of giving proper care, move on to other options. In most cases, everyone will understand and withhold blame. Some caregivers experience a particularly distressing situation: their friends shun them because of the new demands. Losing once supportive relationships can be painful and disillusioning. In some cases, other family members drift out of their lives, leaving a vacuum that is hard to fill.

In summary, use the following rules of thumb:

1. *Balance your responsibilities to your own family.*
   Examine the impact your caregiving has on other members of your family. Personal conflict can cause intense family problems. Work out with each member their expectations and support. Analyze the sacrifices as well as the benefits and try to keep them balanced.

2. *See if you can find a common ground between your work and your caregiving role.*
   Few employers have policies that support workers' needs in caring for aging parents but more companies are becoming concerned as the popu-

lation ages and life expectancy increases. Discuss your situation with appropriate supervisors and work out a plan that allows you to maintain your job and give appropriate care, i.e., flex time, use of vacation and sick leave, and doing some work at home.

3. *Take care that you don't ignore your own needs.*
When a person assumes the care of another, a potential for self-exploitation exists, perhaps unconsciously. Communicate your needs to your parents. Tell them that you will do all you can—it may not be enough, but you must take care of your own responsibilities as well.

4. *Ensure time for yourself.*
Most people realize that private time is essential for one to maintain a positive outlook. Arrange for time to be alone, doing things that you enjoy: a bike ride, a movie, a book, a walk, sports, just being with someone else for a while. Make a conscious effort to keep yourself from becoming isolated, even if it's difficult.

5. *Think toward the future.*
As parents age, their needs change and you need to have a plan that everyone affected agrees to and that can be easily implemented. For most parents, the longer they live, the more complex their dependency becomes, and greater demands are placed on the caregiver. Develop a long-range

plan from beginning care to their final days. Be prepared to change it as necessary. A framework that builds on family strengths can help guide you.

A Quaker Not Given to Idle Threats

I was raised in a small town in northern Minnesota where winter was a condition, not a season. The snow that came to bury our streets and sidewalks was not the white romantic stuff from which the huge winter sports industry sprang, but rather it was the endless, bitter, dangerous snow of the arctic. The thermometer would dip to -20°, go to -30°, and occasionally to -40°, but wherever it was, it sat there. It was pitch-black night when I went to school and when I returned. The snowbanks on both sides of the sidewalks were mounded high over my head and the five-block path to school was a deep, dark trough with exits only at the street intersections. Every child knew that between these intersections lay an untraveled no-man's land, that should anything unseen and terrible befall them there, they would not be seen and would surely freeze. I had no trouble accepting my mortality. It was accomplished in the space between the hospital and the car when my mother and father took me home from the hospital. Anyone who was not completely deranged understood a lot of things after that first encounter with arctic cold. That is why I am confident that not only did they bring home an infant who was totally aware of her mortality, but one who was born hopelessly absentminded. Only individuals who have been affected at a cellular level continue to lose their mittens in -20° or more weather. In this climate the capacity to exfoliate clothing, bitter winter and fragile summer alike, could not *have been an acquired trait.*

I never saw my mother in repose without four knitting needles and a half-made mitten in her hands. She used the brightest yarn she could find, hoping it would make a lost mitten easier to find, but no amount of brightly colored yarn or ignominious threats of being treated like a baby and having my mittens sewn to my snowsuit cuff held up to my condition.

I would lost my mittens somewhere at school. When it came time to come home, I would delay as long as I could, tuck my hands into my armpits, and run for five blocks in what looked like the dead of night and felt like the cold side of hell. My fingers would crack and bleed. My mother would scold. She would threaten. She was a Quaker not given to idle threats, and I was chastened and would promise to be more careful. My mother would knit more furiously.

Mother never did pin or sew my mittens to my cuffs. That would have been a shameful badge to have to carry after the first grade. I had come into this world with some other genetic gifts besides my absentmindedness. I was born with allergies that left me in a sea of snot and wheezes in the summer and wearing a cloak of eczematous scabs in the winter. I'm sure she thought this was quite enough.

Now that she is becoming more and more forgetful, now that I have to answer the same question several times within the space of an endless minute, now that she wishes to hang onto her diminished abilities by what seems like sheer pigheadedness, I must remember the respect she showed me during those years when it would have made her life so much simpler to sew my mittens onto my cuffs and put away her knitting needles.

The self within for the mother and the daughter is revealed in this story. Frequently, when children encounter behaviors in parents as they age that remind them of their own early days, a profound lesson unfolds. But adult children who treat their elderly parents as if they are now the children may reap unintended results—loss of respect by all concerned and a presumed license to abuse and/or manipulate parents. The belief that you are trading places by becoming their parents, while they become the child, is demeaning to them. You may assume tasks similar to those your parents did with you as a child, but they are not your children. They always remain your parents.

CHAPTER 2

Aging in Place and Other Options

Prior to World War II, most Americans expected to age in place—to live in the family home, where they shared the residence with relatives, until death. Few retired to planned communities or nursing homes. Most did not live past seventy years of age. Today, with extended life expectancy, the elderly and their children face new challenges for which they are largely unprepared. Geographic and occupational mobility have rendered many families unattached and transient, so that the system of mutual support no longer exists. Given the choice, most elderly persons would prefer to remain independent and self-reliant, but many are incapable of managing alone. On the other hand, retirement settlements or nursing homes are not always a viable option because of the cost involved. With women outliving men but possessing less wealth, this sector of the population often slips into poverty as they age.

"Where will my aging parent live?" is the question that confronts many an adult. When the following options for living arrangements are studied, financial, medical, social, and personal concerns must be considered:

- Living independently
- Living in their home with assistance from children or paid caregivers
- Homesharing
- The reassembled family—joining the children
- Retirement communities
- Residential care homes
- Nursing homes

Living Independently

Some older parents choose to live independently and to maintain their home, where they feel safe and secure and enjoy the respect given them by society for their vitality and self-sufficiency. In order to opt for this alternative, parents need adequate financial resources, good health, a safe neighborhood, and a stimulating social life. Few manage to remain independent until death, and their children should be aware that the longer their parents live, the more likely it will be that assistance with medical, financial, and social matters will be required. Until such time, children usually encourage their parents' independence and self-reliance.

"How Is Your Mother?"

The daughter beamed proudly, "You won't believe it. She'll outlive us all. I can't keep up with her. Just yesterday I called and she said she'd been wearing a straight shirt all week. 'What does that mean?' I asked. She said she'd been so busy that, as she ran around, her shirttail flew out straight behind her."

"Is she still living in her own home?" the friend inquired.

"Oh, yes. She has lived in the same house for fifty years. She won't live anywhere else. I visit her once a week to take her to the beauty shop and to get groceries. We eat out. She loves that, but she won't come to live with us. I've begged. You know, she'll be ninety-five in April. She makes pear preserves; she picks the pears, rakes the yard, cleans the house, tends her small garden, writes letters regularly, and goes to church three times a week. I don't know how she does it all. She's not as big as a minute."

"How's her health?"

The daughter smiled as she reported, "Excellent. Her hearing is not as good as before, but she wears an aid. Her memory fails once in a while, but her doctors marvel at her energy."

"You're blessed."

Stories like this one inspire and amaze. Few things are more joyful to hear about than that a ninety-five-year-old parent is vital, alert, and lives independently in his/her own home. However, these cases are rare.

Living at Home but Requiring Assistance

The Long Ride

"I've got to drive down to help my folks," Gene says each Saturday morning as he prepares for the regular seventy-mile drive. Although his parents live alone in the family home, they need help.

Gene's father no longer drives, and his mother shows early signs of Alzheimer's. Gene takes his father shopping for groceries, cuts the lawn, helps clean the house, tends to the finances, and enjoys meals and his parents' companionship. It's only a matter of time before they will need closer attention, and he has suggested they move in with him. He worries about their safety, and they worry about becoming a greater burden than they feel they are now.

Each Sunday, on the long drive back to his own family, Gene remembers his childhood, with its share of fun and hurts.

"I'll do the best I can for them. They did for me. But it's so different. They're becoming frail. I can see they wish it were different. But, with my family's help, we'll do the best," he tells his wife and children.

This story is common—adult children helping their parents remain in familiar surroundings and age in place. But many children live great distances from their parents and are simply unable to make regular visits. In these cases, home assistance programs can be arranged and paid caregivers can extend the time in which parents can remain in their own homes. Many community resources are available, and children can help their parents locate them and utilize those with which they feel comfortable. Even though in situations where children cannot be with their aging parents, they can enrich their lives, monitor their health, and protect them financially and legally. While working on these concerns from a distance is a challenge, it is a challenge that many manage.

HELPFUL HINTS

- Talk with your parents. Assure them that you value their independence but want to help if they need or want assistance.
- Visit, phone, or write letters to your parents regularly to assess their ability to remain living independently. Proximity to them eases the stress of not knowing and worrying.
- Ask a neighbor, relative, or friend to keep you informed on their ability to remain safely in their homes.
- Be alert to needs that may develop as they age: transportation, physical fitness, safety and security devices, medical assistance, nutrition, social activities with their peers, financial planning, insurance, and recreation. Try to take care of these needs through private or community agencies providing services to the elderly.

- Encourage them to continue using their talents and to pursue interests that sustained them in the past.

Homesharing

In response to the many changes that have affected the family, a new type of living arrangement has developed over the past twenty years: arranged homesharing. Agencies assume the task of recruiting, matching, and arranging for persons to share a home. Financial, social, medical, and personal constraints make it difficult for many older persons to maintain their home without additional income or caregiver assistance. Homesharing is often not just a solution but also an opportunity for new relationships, either with peers or with a younger family.

One advantage to intergenerational homesharing is that aging parents can arrange for chores such as transportation, yard work, home cleaning, and other physical jobs to be done by the young couple. Having a young couple in the house can stimulate social interaction. Careful matching of the homesharers is of course essential in order to avoid conflicts and disappointments. Going through a shared housing agency can help prevent mistakes and ill-conceived matches.

Not new or uncommon is homesharing among relatives. The decision is usually natural and binding, with older brothers and sisters living together to continue family traditions, to share financial, medical, and safety matters, and to solve the problem of loneliness and isolation.

HELPFUL HINTS

- Encourage your parents to consider homesharing with an appropriate relative, if relationships are positive and reciprocal. Some family members assemble quite naturally, without any encouragement. If exploitation of either party is possible, caution them to consider all the consequences and to be prepared to sever ties if needed. Plan ahead to make a change.

- Visit an agency that provides homesharing services and learn about the program. If you think it presents a viable alternative, discuss it with your parents and obtain their interest. If desired, help with the selection.

- Clarify your parents' expectations to determine if they are realistic about their needs and those of a potential housemate.

- Monitor the homesharing arrangement. Meet the respective tenants and assess the situation with them.

- Set up a trial period in order to get to know one another.

- Explore differences and similarities with potential homesharers in an interview before making a decision.

Take Care of Mary

Al and Larry worked all day planting a new kind of drought-resistant grass. The dry summer had turned their immaculate, green lawn into a coarse brown. Taking care of the yard was one of their chores, while Mary and Louise shopped, cooked, and cleaned house. The four aging Italians had shared the home for more than twenty years. As Al and Larry retired, their routines settled and each knew the other's expectations.

"Take care of Mary," Father had told them when they were young. "You know she is not like others and she'll need your help." Al and Larry knew they would carry out their father's wishes when they bought the house together and brought Al's wife, Louise, and Mary to the small California town.

Each morning, Mary took her broom and swept the sidewalk and the street gutters. Some in the neighborhood thought her peculiar. However, the family protected her.

"When will it get green?" she asked.

"Not until next year. It takes a year to grow; this stuff is slow."

While her brothers worked, Mary continued sweeping in the warm morning sun.

"We've got nothing but time," Larry said with a wry smile. When they finished planting, he'd ride his bicycle to town to get ice cream. Mary shook her head thinking about the grass.

"A whole year before it's green?"

Reassembling

Families reassemble for different reasons: economic, health concerns, death of a spouse, personal preference, or other. Why they reassemble is important and, although no one fully anticipates the demands of this new arrangement, no one should enter into it without a full exploration of the consequences for the parent(s), the child, and other family members. While many surprises cannot be avoided, a realistic appraisal may prevent resentment, guilt, antipathy, and hurt. When the choice is based on mutual personal preference—"we want it this way"—or when it occurs naturally, many obstacles and problems become manageable, and conflicts can be avoided. Living together in this arrangement requires a great deal of time, discussion, and energy. Coming together in a positive, sustaining manner is not always easy.

Because women live longer, have more limited financial means, and can help with nurturing and child care, it is most often the mother who is brought back into the family. Hers has probably been a life of giving to her children, and if the family of her son or daughter has young children, helping with homemaking can be natural and sustaining for both sides. As parents live longer, reassembling often also takes place at the time the child is retired or near retirement.

The following are types of reassembling:

- Parent and child jointly purchase a home, town house, duplex, or mobile home and, while having separate quarters, share meals and other daily activities.
- Parent moves into child's home, has own living area, but helps with family matters and grandchildren if any remain at home.
- Child moves into home of parent, maintains home, and cares for parent.
- Child and parent rent apartment and share life.

A decision to reassemble requires a candid discussion: Do we both want to live together, after many years, and can we make it work? What are we giving up in our present lives if we reunite? Will others in the family agree and support the decision? Why are we doing it?

HELPFUL HINTS
- Let your parents know that, while supporting their independence for as long as possible, a time may come when they need help and you can bring them back into your life rather than going into "assisted living" or a nursing home.
- Realize that bringing the parents back into your life may be expensive and that they may have little, if any, financial resources to contribute. If you are married, make sure that your spouse approves of the arrangement and understands the new demands placed on the family. Many couples break up due to the stress of having to care for an elderly relative. Even stable families can be overwhelmed

and disrupted by daily stress and personality conflicts.

- Be prepared for the onset of diminishing capacity—when aging starts to have a disabling effect. For some, the onset is rapid, for others, slow and nonthreatening.
- Know available community resources that provide assistance and support and allow time away from the demands of a new, aging family member.
- Agree upon useful roles your parent can play such as helping with the household, garden, child care, and part-time work, and encourage the pursuit of hobbies and participation in social events.
- Provide a private area for your parent: a room, an apartment, a portion of a duplex. Having their own area is essential not only for their well-being but also for your need for privacy.
- Share your feelings of joy, anger, pride, confusion, trust, despondency. Suppressing them can lead to deeper interpersonal problems. Say openly: "Mother, there are times I'll be angry and short. I may raise my voice. Accept that in me. And do the same with me because if we're natural and honest we can weather the bad times. Certainly, we'll enjoy the good ones."
- Arrange financial matters to ensure the well-being of the family. Know the resources and how to access them. Remember, if you keep your fragile parent at home, you pay the bills. Medicare and most other insurance policies do not pay for in-home care.
- Keep your own career and occupation as long as

you can. Giving up your own identity is destructive. If you work outside the home, make proper arrangements for caregiving and social contacts for your parent to allow yourself the fulfillment of your needs while protecting your parent from harm and loneliness.

I Was Afraid

"I called my son, William. I was afraid to live alone anymore. I had this terrible fear when my oldest brother died in that fire. His house burned with him in it. He was too old and frail to get out. I thought that could happen to me and Lou. So I called my son and told him I was afraid for us to live alone anymore. He said we should come to California. He'd take care of us. Well, I didn't want to be a burden to his family." Gerard's hands trembled as he recalled the tragedy.

"When we got here, William and Maude had made us this apartment in their home." Gerard waved his arms to point out the three neat rooms that once housed the family's recreation area. Wood-paneled walls were covered with art and family photographs. A large picture of the four Dodge trucks of Green's Transfer Company told the story of their family business in Tampa, Florida, during the early 1900s.

"We came to live with our son and daughter-in-law because I was afraid. He wanted to fix this place up for us, and he did." Gerard rubbed his eyes gently and glanced toward his wife.

"He's happy here," Lou confided.

Gerard leaned back in his big easy chair. "I told Lou

that I would protect her from the world if she would protect me from myself. We've tried."

Turning Back and Finding More

Bernice couldn't believe she was saying yes to this whole thing. Dreams are made of such precarious stuff, but this dream had never soured. Never once in the years since she stepped off the train from Texas had California lost its magic.

It had been five years since the death of Virginia's husband. Bernice and her brothers had agreed that their mother should no longer live alone. So, why had she said yes? There were others there for her mother. There were others and they already lived in Texas. She knew why. Her marriage was over, her daughter was raised and off making a career for herself, and Bernice was the only one who would do things the very best they could be done. Besides, she didn't have a "no" in her. Bernice sold her home, said goodbye to her friends, had a garage sale, gave the rest away, and headed back to Texas.

Both Bernice, the daughter, and Virginia, the mother, had to give up things. Virginia sold her house in Marshall, while Bernice set about finding a new house near Dallas with the capability of providing as much independence as possible for the two of them. She settled on a town house outside of Dallas. She would live upstairs, her mother downstairs—separate but together.

In Los Angeles, Bernice made $12 an hour as a nurse. In Dallas, it would be $8 an hour. She had probably given up the opportunity to remarry. Her church and her Sierra Club were behind her in California. She got a job at Baylor

Hospital and began to work in her new church. They agreed on a once-a-week housekeeper to reconcile housekeeping differences, and a brother took over Virginia's financial affairs. Sometimes Virginia relinquished control over a matter, and sometimes Bernice did. No time for regrets or arguments. There was a life to be led as graciously and happily as God would allow.

Still Talking Southern

"Grandma, it's not dawg—it's dog. Say it again," Phillip instructed his grandmother. She was sitting in the rocking chair, humoring him along. She had come to help her son when Phillip was struggling through a prolonged convalescence following skin graft surgery. In 1974, one day before her eighty-second birthday, she boarded an airplane in the east and flew to California to spend a few weeks as part of a reassembled family, but what were meant to be weeks turned into years. Her one hundredth birthday was celebrated in California in 1991, where she continues to live with her son.

"Dawg. Dawg. Is that right, Phil?"

"No, Grandma. It's dog. You're not trying." Phillip sighed as he issued the entreaty.

"Yes, I am. Dawg," she repeated, without much conviction. Finally, in clipped fashion, she added, "Dag."

"That's better, Grandma. Now, let's try to say 'chair'."

"Cha-yer," Inez uttered slowly.

"No. It's chair."

"I'll never get it right." She smiled. "What's wrong with speaking Southern anyway?" she asked whimsically.

"Grandma, you're in California. We don't pronounce words that way. Now, try again. Say chair."

"Cheer."

Phillip put his arm around his grandmother, acknowledging the impossible task. In a few weeks, he'd travel with his grandmother to Tennessee to spend a summer vacation. In store waiting for him was a town filled with people who said cha-yer, dawg, hep, pra-yer, wagin, and Nash-full. His grandmother would make him the man of the house in her own home, one of many lessons she would provide that were drawn from the wisdom and love growing within her over the years. He'd fix broken windows, run errands, mow the lawn, and replace worn-out light bulbs.

"Do We Have to Go?"

Ida had always said she'd live here the rest of her life. After all, it was the family farmhouse for eighty years. The family members came from the quarry, and the women planted gardens and sewed. Now Ida was alone. Her last brother had just died. The house was far from the town where her only daughter lived. They both feared some untoward event such as a fall or a fire.

Ida, now eighty, stood by the window and looked out at the pear trees and the creek. She remembered springtime in upper New York State and the fish in the creek. The backyard mulberry tree was her secret hideout, where she would climb to the top and watch the men working in the quarry. Now she must sell the house and move to town with her daughter, Kay. They'd buy a mobile home and share the final years.

"Are you ready, Momma?" Kay called out entering the

front door. Ida moved slowly across the room. Her hands and head shook from Parkinson's disease. She leaned on her walking cane. "Do we have to go?"

"Yes, Momma." Tears ran down Kay's cheeks.

They Needed Each Other

Mike's life was falling apart. He was friendless, depressed, and unsure of the future. Acute anxiety overwhelmed him. At forty, he felt adrift and out-of-touch with his activist colleagues of the Vietnam protest era. As they became mainstream, he found little affinity with anyone. Finally, he snapped and was hospitalized for depression. On the long road to recovery, Mike made a decision—he would go home. Leaving Seattle was difficult but he needed to find meaning in his life and a place to mend.

"Stay with us," his mother said when he arrived home for the first time in many years. "We need you." They did. The years were taking their toll. Mike's parents, in their seventies, had changed. Mike had changed also. His father had heart trouble, diabetes, and was withdrawn— unlike the once gregarious man Mike knew. His mother, a reserved person with advanced osteoarthritis, was unable to cook, take care of the house, or cope with her failing health. Mike noticed how frail she was. The changes saddened him, cutting deeper into his already broad despair.

"Why did I come home?" he asked himself many times during the first few months. At night, he lay awake for hours, mulling over the decision. Slowly, almost without realizing it, Mike assumed new duties. He began to cook, shop, clean the house, drive his parents, handle the family

finances, tend to the laundry, garden, and take his parents to Mass each Sunday. He read while they watched television. Mike joined a local peace group.

Over the past three years, this quiet family pulled together, each remaining unable to speak about the change, but aware that a fragile security has grown to halt the disintegration of their Irish Catholic family. The three are bound in mutual vulnerability. No one is truly happy— the old couple's health diminishes and their isolation from the community increases. Mike finds solace in his new cause but no joy. Simply, they need each other.

Retirement Communities

The elderly who enjoy a good income have far more options than those whose retirement income places them near poverty. And few children can subsidize expensive retirement for their elderly parents. Financial and health concerns dictate the type of retirement home they will choose.

Many different types of residential retirement communities are available to your parents. Check them out and encourage them to select one that's affordable and appealing.

Continuing Care Retirement Communities. Many parents who want to or find they must sell their homes have turned to continuing care retirement communities. These facilities typically offer no ownership position but provide residential, leisure, and nursing services in exchange for large, nonrefundable entrance fees and a monthly payment. A few provide an equity stake but no health care, while others will help with bathing, dressing, and taking medication on a fee-for-service basis. While those built twenty years ago were mostly operated as not-for-profit, recently built ones may be operated by profit-making corporations, such as a hotel chain or a medical group.

When seeking a facility, discuss the decision with your parents. Unforeseen problems can be prevented.

HELPFUL HINTS

- Know tax implications. Most home sellers can shelter the first $125,000 of capital gain; however, they may be responsible for a large substantial income tax if the house value is substantial. When a large up-front payment is required to move into a retirement community, determine whether you can obtain an ownership interest.

- Consider parents' special needs. Some parents may want to be free of all household responsibilities, while others many find they miss living in their own home and doing the chores. They may dislike the barracklike atmosphere of congregate living. Others may have health problems and need care. Be sure the facility of choice can provide health care. Many retirement communities require the residents to be in good health before they move in and that they carry full Medicare insurance (Parts A and B). In addition, they need to have either their own supplemental insurance or pay into a supplemental group policy for long-term care.

- Consult an attorney before making a decision about entry into a life-care facility. Many contracts are inappropriate, inequitable, and possibly unlawful. In addition, the solvency of the project owner and management must be checked. Some bankruptcies have occurred, leaving the purchasers or renters in financial trouble. Carefully examine the contract terms to ensure the safety of your parents' deposit.

- Know levels of care. Some continuing care facilities provide three levels of care. They offer independent living for those elderly who are fully functional, assisted living for those who need help dressing or getting out of bed, and, finally, the nursing home. All three levels may be contained within the same facility. Fees for each differ, but, as the level of care increases, so do the fees.

- Understand financial demands. Many residents live in fear that their money will not last as long as they live, and they wonder what will happen when their resources are depleted. Large for-profit complexes are certain to face these problems as people live longer and have more serious medical needs.

- Discuss your concerns with residence managers.

Continuing care homes attract mostly widowed women aged seventy-nine and older who have never lived in these arrangements before. They are often afraid and confused. Giving up their independence and familiar surroundings can be traumatic.

Low-cost subsidized housing. In some urban areas, continuing care services are available to poor older people in government subsidized housing complexes. Check out their requirements. They are designed to prevent the elderly from being placed in a nursing home simply on the grounds that they can no longer manage to live independently but need no special medical services.

Board and Residential Care Homes

Residential care facilities vary in size, number of residents, health requirements, and fees. They are licensed by the State Health Department, and each type has different regulations. They are privately operated, and monthly rent is assessed. Some are expensive; others are moderately priced. Medicare and Medicaid do not cover these group homes, making the family responsible for all costs.

Six-patient care facilities create a homelike environment that tends to emotional, intellectual, and social needs. They do not provide in-house nursing or medical care. Family members are usually responsible for taking their parents for medical appointments. Some homes are licensed for ambulatory patients only; others for bedridden and wheelchair residents. Three meals are served each day at a dining room table. Each patient has a private room. A game room, patio, and living room are usually provided. Care includes meals, assistance with eating, recreation, assistance with dressing and bathing, medication monitoring, linen and laundry service, and supervision.

Residential care facilities for more than six patients are available in many communities. They can accept from seven to as many as one hundred and fifty elderly residents. Admission requirements vary. Larger facilities usually offer more activities for the elderly, but they become less homelike as their population increases. Residents rent their rooms and receive all care except medical attention. Medicare and Medicaid are not accepted.

HELPFUL HINTS

- Make an unannounced visit, preferably at meal time, to inspect the facility prior to placing your parent there. If the staff does not feel comfortable with your unannounced visit, you should consider a different place. You will learn about the nutrition and quality of service provided. Talk with the staff and observe the residents' appearance and demeanor. Observe how crises are handled.
- Discuss the size of the population with your parent and choose the residential facility that meets their need. Some like the larger facilities because of the varied activities; others prefer a quieter, more homelike atmosphere.
- Be prepared to pay for the care. Monthly rents vary, and you will not receive financial assistance from public agencies.

- Know the types of care offered and select the one that serves your parents' health, emotional, and social needs.
- Read the latest evaluation from the licensing authority—the State Department of Health—in order to know the history and current status of the facility. Ask questions about violations of regulations.
- Find out how medical emergencies are handled.
- Be prepared to provide transportation to medical and other appointments.
- Volunteer, if you have time, to help with social activities.

Nursing Homes (Convalescent Hospitals)

One of the most difficult decisions a child and parent can be forced to make is the placement of the elderly parent in a nursing home. Old people dread it, and their children may feel sad and guilty. Institutional settings (nursing homes, mental hospitals, prisons) share certain problems. Inmates or residents, as well as the people operating the institution, may experience the same psychological conversion. Pride and self-respect are injured and, over time, a certain callousness to their own feelings as well as others' is unavoidable. The spirit tends to die as they become creatures of routine and denial. Children should be aware of the dying process and work to prevent it or, if there are warnings signs, help their parents cope.

Today, nearly two million Americans reside in nursing homes, with only a small fraction ever again returning to another place of residence. Most residents are women. Very alarming is the fact that fully one quarter of the residents in this type of institution have no medical reason for being there. The average cost per year is $30,000 and some go as high as $80,000. Medicare does not pay for long-term care in a nursing home nor do most private insurance carriers.

Nursing homes usually have a mixed reputation. Various, sometime euphemistic names are used for nursing care institutions. While some reform is being made, both from within and under pressures from the outside, they remain problematic. State Health Departments license them and provide periodic inspections. However, violations occur:

- More than seventy percent of patients are controlled by powerful psychotropic drugs. Facilities often turn to milder drugs if they cannot document or defend the use of psychotropic drugs.
- According to facility managers, many patients are restrained in their wheelchairs with belts and vests that keep them from falling.
- At least one quarter of nursing homes have been cited for violations in food preparation and storage, failure to follow proper medication procedures, and failure to provide proper hygiene and dental care. Others are cited for failure to give residents with urinary catheters routine care and periodic evaluation, care and rehabilitation training with

bowel or bladder control problems, and exercise to prevent paralysis or loss of ability to walk or move.

If you find there is no alternative to placing your parent in a nursing home, you need to closely monitor the situation. Nursing home care is expensive. It can also be emotionally wrenching, but at times there may be no alternative.

HELPFUL HINTS
- Visit several nursing homes in the area and ask questions about their use of medication and restraints to control patients. Walk around and get a feeling for the quality of care offered. Select the institution you feel most confident about.
- Check with the Department of Health. In most states, the most recent inspection report is available for public access. Check records of violations. Read the report and discuss it with nursing home staff.
- Determine the cost of nursing home care. Medicare usually only pays for it after hospitalization and for a limited number of days. Learn what to expect from both Medicare and your parent's supplemental insurance.
- Be prepared to assume extra costs. Most nursing homes provide extra services, usually for a fee.
- Observe the following indications of poor care in nursing homes:
  —smell of urine in hallways;
  —restraints used to confine residents;
  —rashes caused by improper laundering;

    —poor dental care and improper hygiene;
    —dirty clothing;
    —bed sores.

- Talk with nursing aids to encourage them to give your parent personal attention. Tell them about the things your parent likes, such as music, reading materials, conversation, and so on.
- Check the menu and verify that the one posted is actually given to the residents.
- Bring gifts occasionally to staff members who tend your parent.
- Ensure your parent's proper grooming. For your mother, have a hairdresser come in; for your father, provide a barber to shave and give a haircut.
- Place your telephone number by your parent's bed and ask the staff to call you if there is a serious problem.
- Help out with personal care when you visit, if appropriate.
- Talk with other visitors to assess their opinion of the care their loved one is receiving.
- Place photographs of family members in your parent's room. A person with the appearance of being cared for by a family may receive better care.
- Use the nursing home ombudsman if you suspect a problem between your parent and the staff.
- Learn about the conditions under which Medicaid (welfare) pays for your parent's stay. Most states require that your parent disposes of personal assets prior to being eligible for assistance. Medicaid pays

up to $1,500 a month in some states, but your parent must be at the poverty level to qualify.

- Check into Supplemental Security Income (SSI). Your parent may be eligible for SSI to provide additional needed income if financial resources are inadequate. SSI varies from state to state.
- Be prepared to supplement the Medicare payment for your parent's stay in a nursing home. Extra amenities can be purchased in many of them.
- Ensure that the facility has provisions to accept a living will and durable power of attorney for health care. They are required by law to recognize and implement them.
- Visit as often as possible because patients generally feel isolated and depressed and need contact with family and friends. Nursing homes can be lonely and frightening places. Many patients receive no visitors and die alone.

Sell the Home

When her mother could care for herself no longer, Jane brought her from the Midwest to live with her. For several years, the mother was able to help out around the house. Then, senility and a series of falls began to take their toll. Jane had promised to take care of her mother and had every intention of keeping her word. As her mother required constant attention and she worked long hours, Jane hired an aide to come during the day, but the costs were edging her toward bankruptcy.

"I need help to keep my mother at home," she told the Medicare worker, who informed her that Medicare would

pay nothing if she kept her mother at home. On the other hand, all basic expenses would be paid for if she put her in a nursing home. A requirement was that her mother sell the small home she owned back in Ohio. Those were the rules.

"Mom, I don't want to do it. But we have no other choice," Jane told her mother, who hardly understood the consequences, for which Jane was glad.

Taking her to the nursing home was the hardest thing she ever did, Jane told her friends.

CHAPTER 3

---◆---

Health Care—
Primary Concerns

Aging is often accompanied by a series of chronic health problems. As time goes on, these tend to accelerate, especially once the seventh decade has been reached. Not surprisingly, the widely held view is that growing old is to be dreaded because it will bring frailty, illness, and a loss of vitality. The natural degeneration of the body *can* make older people more susceptible to cancer, stroke, diabetes, arthritis, depression, falls, and Alzheimer's disease, and the misuse of prescription medication, over-the-counter drugs, improper diet, smoking, alcohol, and social isolation can make it hard for them to cope with everyday life.

Is it within our power to make their last years physically and emotionally less taxing? Can adult children help make longer lives better lives for their parents? Can we lessen their fears of terminal illness or of ending up painstricken, abandoned, with no hope for relief or comfort? The answer is YES. There is almost no limit to the ways in which we can enhance aging, even in the face of illness and increasing dependence.

Prevention and health promotion are first priorities. Immediate and proper medical attention has to be obtained whenever a health problem manifests itself. If the elderly are unable to arrange for it, it falls to the family to do it for them. In addition to professional medical care, you can do a number of things to help.

Keeping Fit

Exercise lowers cholesterol and blood pressure. People not only gain strength and look better from exercising, they also report that it boosts their spirits. Yet, few people over fifty engage in some form of vigorous exercise.

According to recent articles in medical journals, modest exercising substantially reduces the chances of fatal heart disease, cancer, or some chronic illnesses. Exercise reduces the chances of adult diabetes, a disease that afflicts more than twelve million Americans. People in the highest risk group—those with a family history of diabetes, those who are overweight, and those suffering from hypertension—benefit the most from an exercise program that prevents the onset of the disease. While exercise alone will obviously not completely prevent these diseases, it will reduce certain risk factors. Much of what appears to be aspects of aging, such as declining muscle strength, fatigue, and weight gain, now seems to be the result of a mostly sedentary life.

With strengthened heart and lungs, people don't tire as easily, and physical activity helps your parents keep their independence longer. Weak muscles contribute to falls and the failure to keep up with routine daily activities. The elderly find that being stronger allows them to lift grocery bags, climb stairs, get in and out of cars, dress, bathe, and prepare for bed—things that enhance their sense of well-being and self-respect. Some experts say that exercise is not a luxury—it's essential.

HELPFUL HINTS

- Discuss an exercise regime with them and appropriate medical authorities.
- Discuss their using safe exercise equipment, such as weights and a stationary bicycle to build and maintain muscle tone and endurance.
- Encourage them to take walks in the neighborhood with a companion. Learn to gauge appropriate distance and plan a safe route.
- Help them take advantage of physical exercise and aerobics programs provided at senior centers or for seniors at other locations, such as the neighborhood gym or pool.
- Encourage them to feel proud of their athletic abilities and continue to participate as long as it's appropriate.

The Bicycle

When Virginia was a girl, she thought that someday she would own a bicycle and rise across west Texas. It was flat enough, and there were some long country roads to travel.

Today, Virginia owns a bicycle—not the kind you take outside. Hers is an exercise machine that sits on a platform in her bedroom. Every day Virginia does her workout, pumping the pedals and going nowhere—except in her imagination.

"Momma gets her exercise. Her legs are strong and, at ninety-seven, she walks everywhere. Did you know that she can still bend and touch her palms to the floor? I can't do that. She just starting using a walking cane recently." Bernice glanced at the bike almost fondly. As a nurse, she knows the importance of regular exercise and encourages her mother.

"You're never too old to ride a bicycle," Virginia says.

Learn How to Bathe and Dress Your Parent

Millions of older Americans require assistance with bathing and dressing each day. Essential, on the part of the assisting child, are good organization skills and a great respect for the need for privacy. Unless children are conscious of their parents' vulnerability, loss of dignity and independence can occur. But taking care of these personal needs can also be physically demanding. To avoid conflict and help overcome resistance, a direct and caring discussion with the parent to assess what is to be done and how to do it can be fruitful. Initially, your involvement in these intimate acts will be somewhat frightening, no matter how well prepared both of you think you are. Assume responsibility for bathing and dressing your aging parents only when they can no longer to it themselves.

HELPFUL HINTS
- Select an appropriate place to give the bath, perhaps at the bedside or in the bathroom. Choose a warm and comfortable spot with easy access to all needed items. Use a safe place with ample room to move about.
- Use warm water from the shower or hot water if you use pans for a sponge bath. Water in pans gets cold quickly.
- Decide who bathes each part of the body and encourage the parent to do as much bathing as possible.
- Have three washcloths and a towel available. If the parent is soiled, discard the washcloth after wiping and use a fresh one to complete the bath.
- Agree upon a regular time for the bath. An early morning one allows an opportunity for the bath and dressing together, and a full day of freshness.
- Use plastic covering to protect the floor and/or rugs around the bed if that's the chosen location. If the parent in incontinent, remove the wet bedding. Protective plastic sheets and mattress covers ensure a sanitary, comfortable sleeping area.

- Use lotion generously to prevent dry and chapped skin. Watch for rashes, bed sores, and other abrasions and bruises and obtain necessary treatment immediately when skin ailments are identified. Infections spread quickly in elderly people.
- Obtain advice from a pharmacy regarding extra-sensitive skin and special soaps. Antiseptic soaps that require no rinsing are good for those who are incontinent. These medicated, concentrated liquid soaps are good for cleaning urine and feces from the body, linens, and other soiled areas.
- Organize the bathing area before the task commences. Have a towel, washcloths, and a chair to hold onto as the person rises to dress. If a shower is used, consider shower chairs and safety railings. Have all clothing nearby and dress the parent as the bathing proceeds from head to toe. Have a dressing robe available. Never bathe or dress in a drafty, cold area.
- Clean dentures daily and provide overnight soaking.
- Wash hair as often as necessary, especially if the parent is incontinent. Shampoos can be given at the kitchen or bathroom sink where ample warm water is available.
- Cut fingernails and toenails regularly. Watch for corns and other irregularities of the feet and hands. Obtain treatment when indicated.
- Make bathing and dressing as positive as possible. Play music, watch television, or talk. Encourage the parent to participate fully.

- Shop around at medical supply stores to learn about valuable aids, such as potty chairs, shower chairs, toilet seat cushions, safety railings, and other devices to provide safety and comfort.
- Purchase a lifting belt from a hardware store to protect your back from injury in the event you need to lift your parent.
- Remember, the essential items are:
  —three washcloths;
  —a bath towel;
  —liquid soap;
  —hot or warm water;
  —two one-gallon pails for a sponge bath;
  —chairs for showers.

The Bath by the Bed

"I came to watch great-grandmother get out of bed," four-year-old Lindsay announced as she confidently walked down the long hallway, following closely behind her great-uncle. The night before, members of the family had assembled to celebrate Inez Adams's ninety-ninth birthday. Lindsay was one of six great-grandchildren who had come with her family from Colorado to California to see her great-grandmother for the first time on this special occasion. Her curiosity was keen.

"It takes a while for her to get out of bed. She takes a bath first," her great-uncle replied as they entered the room where the woman slept. Inez lay awake in bed as sunlight streamed through the light curtains.

"Can I watch her take a bath?" Lindsay begged.

"We'll ask Mother." He went to the bed. "Mother,

Lindsay came to see you get up. She wants to watch you take a bath. Is that okay?"

Inez, a shy and modest person by nature, thought for a moment. "All right, if you think it's all right."

"I do," the son replied. Lindsay sat on a chair near the bed and observed every action.

Since a fall in the bathroom eight months earlier, Inez now took a sponge bath each morning at her bed. Two large pans of hot water, one with liquid soap and one without to rinse were placed on a chair by the bed, a chair she held onto as she stood to wash the front of her body. Her son washed the back of her body and placed her garments around her neck as they proceeded with the daily ritual.

"Have you ever seen false teeth before, Lindsay?"

"No. What are they?" The child's eyes grew big.

"I've had these for 67 years. Dr. Harris pulled all my teeth in one day. I walked home from his office. Then he made me this upper plate." She showed the ancient dentures to the intrigued young girl, who examined them carefully.

"They're old. How much did you pay for them?"

"Your great-grandfather made a twin bed of cherry wood for Dr. Harris. It was beautiful. We did things that way—to pay for things. He made fine furniture. I've had these all these years. Dr. Harris did fine dental work. Wiley made fine furniture. They were perfectionists."

"They're old." Lindsay rested her chin on her hands as she watched her great-grandmother place the dentures in her mouth and dry herself before she pulled the slip and dress down over her body. She sat on the side of the bed and put on her stockings and soft shoes, while her son removed the pans of water and wet clothing.

"You forgot to comb your hair," Lindsay called out.

"I did, didn't I? Would you like to help?"

"Yes, yes." She rushed to the bed, took the comb, and ran it through her great-grandmother's fine white hair. "It's so beautiful. I like your white hair, Great-grandmother."

"Now, let's get Mother in her travel chair and go have some breakfast." Lindsay's great-uncle Tom helped his mother from the bed to her travel chair.

"Do you do this every morning?" Lindsay inquired.

"Yes. Mother can't do it alone. She helps. Well, how does she look?"

"Great!" Lindsay rose from the chair and watched as the exchange was made from the bed to the chair. She moved to her great-uncle and pulled at his shirt to get his attention. "I hope great-grandmother lives to be twenty-hundred years old!"

Inez laughed softly. "That's a long, long time, honey." Lindsay bolted from the room and dashed down the hall-way.

As Inez sat at the table, drinking her two cups of hot coffee, she was suddenly surrounded by five small children.

"We came to see great-grandmother take a bath in bed," Laurie said excitedly.

"Do you really take a bath in bed?" Nick, a great-grandson, asked. They gathered around the chair and urged an answer. Their hands reached out to touch the gentle woman.

"Lindsay said she got to watch you take a bath in bed." Laurie hoped her plea would be answered.

Inez turned to the eager children and calmly replied, "Tomorrow. I only take one a day. So you can help me tomorrow, if you want."

Food, Food, Food

Some people live healthily into their nineties—even past one hundred—declaring that it's the whiskey and the cigars that did it while others are felled in their fifties by strokes and heart attacks. They may have never smoked or missed a day of Sunday school. As we learn each year, nutrition and aging are both a study of change. What changes brought on by aging affect nutrition? The list is long and clear.

PHYSIOLOGICAL CHANGES
- Teeth are frequently damaged by decay or periodontal diseases, and many wear dentures or nothing, thus affecting what is eaten.
- Saliva lessens, making chewing and swallowing more difficult.
- Less hydrochloric acid is secreted in the stomach, and digestive enzymes in the stomach and small intestines diminish, thus changing the digestive process.
- The loss of muscle tone slows elimination and, after years of diet deficient in fiber, some muscles along the digestive tract may atrophy and further inhibit proper elimination.
- Senses (taste, smell, sight) may diminish, making food uninteresting.

SOCIAL CHANGES
- Reduced finances affect food choices.
- Loneliness affects eating problems.
- Fear of violence may inhibit the trip to a grocery store.

CHANGES IN NUTRITIONAL NEEDS
- The body requires fewer calories and more fiber (complex carbohydrates).
- Men, and women in particular, require more calcium.
- Women require less iron and folic acid than they did during their child-bearing years.
- More chromium is needed to aid glucose metabolism.
- Those on diuretics for hypertension require more potassium.
- Those who smoke or drink to excess (more than two drinks a day) deplete their vitamins and minerals.

Diet is an area of life in which people can exert a maximum of control; however, most people are tied to their habits and find it difficult to change. If you feel your parents' health is affected by their diet, you can help.

HELPFUL HINTS
- Check the refrigerator when visiting your parents. What looks old? Replace it with fresh food.
- Bring food in two portions—one for a shared meal and one for a later time.

- Check the food your parents eat if they receive Meals On Wheels dinners. Many of these meals are heavy on fats. Ask for vegetables.
- Keep fresh fruit and vegetables in the house. Cut up apples, carrots, and celery in small slices and put in plastic bags. If they are too hard to eat, steam them and shower them with lime or lemon juice, chopped raisins, and spices.
- Make a batch of sauces and freeze them in plastic packets. They can be used with rice, pastas, potatoes, and other vegetables.
- Encourage your parents to eat popcorn, but watch out for excessive salt and oils.
- Do not take away favorite foods, unless they are dangerous to your parents' health. Just reduce the portions, discuss the disadvantages, and try to introduce substitutes.
- Encourage your parents to drink filtered water.
- Avoid artificial flavors and colors, sodium, too many refined sugars, red meat, too much protein, saturated fats, and most dairy products.
- Avoid nagging your parents about their eating habits.
- Eat together as often as possible. Encourage your parents to enjoy a hot meal at the senior center. In some cases, with whom you are eating is more important that what you are eating.
- Learn the Heimlich maneuver. Be careful to avoid breaking ribs. Older people have a high risk of choking and the lack of oxygen can cause permanent brain damage or death.

Eat and Be Merry

Mark quickly and deliberately moves down the super-market aisles. Delayed at work, he is later than usual. He reaches for the shopping list but is unable to locate it. He feels vaguely depressed and tries to concentrate on what to have for dinner.

"One day at a time," that's what the AA sticker says. He thinks, "These people kicked a substance so powerful the state has seen fit to regulate it." Apples, lettuce, pasta, juice go into the cart. Frozen entrées beckon. He gives in to two Budget Gourmet dishes: Italian Lasagna and Sweet and Sour. He has a habit of using just a quarter at a time, chopping them up. To the Italian Lasagna, he normally adds basil and oil, and the Sweet and Sour gets lots of chopped vegetables. He only occasionally uses the frozen entrées for flavoring. The amount of cheese is negligible; moreover, it's time someone else cooks, he decides.

Once at the checkout stand, Mark realizes he has forgotten the popcorn but doesn't go back to get it. Looking around at the other shoppers, he wonders how many of them are middle-aged children rushing home to parents? How many in this store cook meals, clean up, and help their parents into a bed from which they may not rise in the morning? He has seen them before: gray, worn women pushing their mothers in wheelchairs. He feels good about having arranged, just last week, with the nearby church to have a woman come one night a week to stay with his mother. Now he can go have a drink at his old bar and, maybe, go to a movie.

Mark loves his mother, but taking care of her certainly isn't easy now that she is getting so old. All the energy and time it takes may cause him to grow old and worn before his time. This is something neither his mother nor he wants to happen. Who knows when it will be necessary to stay at home all day as well as all night? He shudders.

By the time Mark gets home, the automatic timer has turned on the lights. He enters the house as the news anchor bids good night to the woman asleep before the TV set.

Ruth, who used to make certain that her son received the necessary vitamins and minerals, now needs encouragement to eat what's good for her. Mark has devised ways to turn high fiber into spaghetti marinara, and beans and rice into senior wingdinger specials with homemade salsa. He wants it for his own health also. The red meats and cheeses and creams have disappeared. Rich desserts are replaced with fruits. The slow transition was made together, and they prefer it that way.

The drink they have together is another matter. "How about a little health food bourbon?" Mark wants to know. They sit down to review the day over a drink. The evening drink is a ritual that neither considers giving up.

"They say it's good for you—one a day." Ruth watches her son empty the jigger into her glass.

"Well, chemically, it's like formaldehyde; you know that's true."

"Just one," Ruth comments, "they say one's good for you," forgetting she just said that.

"Let's exchange notes on how the world went to hell today."

Mark and Ruth often have TV dinners on trays. Still in front of the TV, Ruth wipes the trays with a damp cloth that Mark has handed her and then tosses the crumpled paper napkins skillfully into the kitchen wastebasket. Hav-

ing played basketball as a young woman, Ruth once boasted of her ability to make perfect ringers with objects tossed into wastebaskets from great distances. Now, her hoop consists of the top portion of a tomato frame which Mark inserted into the kitchen wastebasket, and every time she makes a shot, Mark applauds.

Mark has seen other parents grow old, without humor. Ruth knows her son stands between her and a nursing home.

Consider Installing a Help-Alert System

Elderly parents and their children share a similar fear—that something dangerous will occur and no one will be there to respond to the crisis. Persistent fears are: falling in the bathroom and lying unattended and unnoticed for hours or days; being burglarized or assaulted and having precious belongings taken; and having a fire that destroys the house and injures or kills the trapped, elderly parent(s). For some, these fears have already been realized. However, feeling helpless in the face of danger can be overcome.

Finding peace of mind and a sense of security is important to parents and their children. When elderly parents choose to, or must, remain alone for long periods, they are vulnerable to a series of misfortunes. Many cannot use the telephone to obtain assistance when an untoward event occurs. Often the circumstances may prevent summoning help: a fall may cause unconsciousness; a sudden fire or the intrusion of a burglar may be paralyzing.

Installing an electronic system that provides immediate access to professional assistance can be very helpful. The parent feels more protected, and the caregiver, knowing that help is within reach, feels safe leaving the parent alone. The pressures produced by constant care can be partially alleviated. Even children whose elderly parents maintain their own homes or apartments may wish to encourage the installation of an alert system.

HELPFUL HINTS

- Consider installing an alert system (commercial) that provides immediate access to fire and police departments and emergency medical services. When being able to use the 911 number is difficult, an electronic system is desirable.
- Follow these procedures:
  —Understand the system and explain it to the elderly parent.
  —Maintain the batteries, conduct regular tests of the system, and track its use.
  —Provide a pendant or wristband that is worn at all times with a button to press to activate the system.
  —Agree upon an entry to the house or apartment to be used by those responding to the call and ensure that it is functional (an unlocked back window or a key with a neighbor).
  —Alert the neighbors that a system has been installed.

- Contact the parent by telephone at prescribed times to reassure and assess their safety.
- Leave a note with a telephone contact where you can be reached in an emergency.
- Arrange for someone to care for your parent if you are away for an extended period of time. Make certain the caregiver is trained, reliable, and concerned. If possible, ask a friendly neighbor to drop by to visit and check up.
- Install locks and chains to prevent unlawful entries and to assure parents that they are safe.
- Check with a telephone company to discuss their many services, such as automated calling, frequently used numbers, and answering machines. Telephone services for persons with diminished capacity are available and new ones are being developed.
- Remove throw rugs that can cause your parent to slip and fall.
- Make sure sharp objects are not near the path they travel.
  —Keep a light on at night, usually in the bathroom, to notify prospective intruders that the house is occupied. Some people install programmed lights that activate at intervals.
  —Keep a flashlight at the bedside of the elderly parent. Falls in a darkened room are common.

We Can't Find You

"Mrs. Adams, Inez, where are you? We've come to help," the fire chief called out as he entered the room through the

slightly opened window by the bed. Following him was a medic. They looked about the room and briskly hurried throughout the house, seeking the woman who had pushed the distress button on her help-alert system. Their records showed she was ninety-seven years old, and the agreed-upon entry was through the slightly opened back window. The system, purchased two years earlier, had never been used before.

"Mrs. Adams, Mrs. Adams. Are you all right? We can't find you," the fire chief repeated. The help-alert system had been installed by Inez's son as protection in case of fire, medical emergency, or robbery when he was away.

Staying alone caused Inez some apprehension, and she and her son felt secure knowing help was only minutes away with the new device. She wore a pendant around her neck at all times, and one quick press on the button in the middle brought immediate help.

"I'm in here." The muffled cry issued from the closet in her room. Inez lay against some boxes, unhurt.

The men expressed relief when they finally found her. "Are you okay? Are you hurt?"

"No, I'm fine, I think. I'm embarrassed for you to find me in here. I don't want all this attention."

Inez had fallen into the closet reaching for her gown when she was changing for bed. Her son was away for a few hours, and she reckoned it was necessary to call for help for the first time since the help-alert system had been installed. She was embarrassed at being found in the closet. As the men lifted her and placed her on the bed, she continued to apologize. "I shouldn't have taken up your time like this. I'm not hurt. After I called, I was ashamed *for you to find me like this. I thought if I just stayed quietly in the closet, you'd go away."*

"That's okay, Mrs. Adams. At least you're okay. No broken bones. Were you afraid?"

"Some. But now I know this gadget works. I feel fine. You're nice men to come so quickly."

The fire chief reassured her. "Do you have a neighbor I can talk with?"

"Yes, Mrs. Johnson directly across the street." Inez knew Mrs. Johnson would help her.

"I'll get her to stay with you for a while. You'll be fine." He left the medic standing by the bed.

"I'm so embarrassed. Don't tell my son about this." Inez reached out to the medic.

"We won't. You just rest now. Okay?"

Some Memory Loss is Inevitable

Loss of memory occurs with age, gradually or, often, dramatically, as in Alzheimer's disease. Most memory loss cannot be reversed; however, those who care for elderly parents can apply techniques to mitigate the effects and an accompanying sense of defeat. Living with a person whose memory is failing can be trying and frustrating, evoking anger at times. The caregiver may confuse memory loss with a lack of attentiveness on the part of the parent and feel neglected. Persons with hearing loss may become confused when they do not hear or understand what's being said to them.

People who regularly take medication and have memory problems should check with their physician to learn if there is any relationship. Some aging parents feel anxiety about their loss of memory; instead of being patient until they do remember, they get upset with themselves.

Few conditions affecting the elderly parent produce as much distress as a loss of memory. Children feel deprived of their familial relationship as they notice their parents struggling to maintain recognition, coherence, and even simple thoughts that once were taken for granted. To lose a sense of the past is painful, both for the parent and the child. The most acute memory loss comes with Alzheimer's disease.

Alzheimer's Disease
During the last ten years, older Americans have been haunted by Alzheimer's disease. Some call it America's greatest new public health dilemma. Ten percent of the population between sixty-five and eighty-five acquire it, while fifty percent of those over eighty-five become afflicted. The illness strikes the aging by destroying brain cells, which results in memory loss, impaired cognition, and ultimately affects the physical functioning. The brain loses acetylcholine, a necessary chemical for brain cell transmissions. Causes and cure are unknown as yet; however, recent research suggests possible links to a virus, toxins, or genetic inheritance. The fourth leading killer of elderly adults, it takes 100,000 lives a year.

Alzheimer's disease is largely misunderstood. Contrary to myths, it is not a normal part of aging, nor does it evolve as a result of the hardening of arteries. It is a disease, fatal and incurable, that can run a course of six to twenty years, during which the patient gradually loses most mental and emotional abilities. It creates great emotional, physical, and financial strains for patients, as well as for their families. The final stages bring an increased chance of contracting pneumonia or other infections that lead to the often bedridden patient's demise. Watching the patient deteriorate is painful for family and friends. More than seventy percent of the patients remain at home, and, in most cases, family members care for them, often with little or no knowledge or understanding of this disease. Some elderly patients wander about, become depressed, or experience uncontrollable outbursts of anger or violence. As they become incontinent and can neither feed nor dress themselves, pressures mount on family caregivers.

Alzheimer's disease is shrouded in mystery and evokes great fear among the elderly and their families. While there is no cure, some symptoms can be treated, but family caregivers require much information, support, and understanding in order to manage this devastating illness.

HELPFUL HINTS

- Be patient and calm and repeat and clarify when necessary.
- Prepare lists of things to be remembered, and encourage the elderly person to do likewise. If the parent's vision is good, give them the list for constant reference. One list may be "Things to Do

73

Today.'' Lists should be simple, short, and useful. They can check off each accomplishment.

- Develop easy-to-follow routines, especially for important things like taking medication. Encourage them to select the routine that's most effective, i.e., counting out a week's supply of pills and placing them in a dispenser.

- Have your parent's regular correspondents enclose self-addressed, stamped envelopes in their letters to facilitate a reply. This helps the elderly avoid long searches for old envelopes to obtain a forgotten address. As with anyone else, a response to a bill or letter is more likely if an envelope is enclosed.

- Find appropriate occasions to discuss the past with them, for instance, when bathing, dressing, or dining. Accept that the same story may be repeated many times. Encourage reminiscence by actively questioning and responding. Short-term memory is likely to diminish first. While struggling with the present, many older people are lucid about the past.

- Become the current memory only when necessary, and encourage them to sort out people, places, and times if the process does not frustrate and irritate.

- Prepare to assume such responsibilities as paying bills, maintaining financial obligations, and ensuring the administration of prescribed medication when their memory loss jeopardizes well-being.

- Avoid, if possible, angry emotional outbursts with forgetful parents because anger only complicates an already difficult situation.

- Contact appropriate organizations and talk with their physicians if Alzheimer's disease is diagnosed.

Just a Baby

"America's just a baby. It's so young in the scheme of things. You take India and China—they had centuries to go by to learn how they wanted their people to be. But America, it's still just a baby. It hasn't learned how to treat its old people. We're still afraid of them. In China, they respect their elders and cherish their wisdom. We put our old folks away, out of sight. But, Momma, I do believe that this great country of ours will learn someday." Bernice turned to look at her mother as they sat and talked at the kitchen table.

"I just don't know how you did it during the Depression. It was so hard," Bernice continued.

Virginia watched tears form in her daughter's eyes. *"Well, I have two things left—a strong voice and a good appetite. They'll get me by, I reckon. Them and prayers. I've always trusted in the Lord. My memory's not what it used to be,"* Virginia continued.

Bernice sat silently as she remembered that her mother had lapses of memory. One day, Bernice came into the kitchen to find her mother at the coffeepot saying, *"I can't remember. I just can't remember how to make coffee anymore."*

Bernice went to her side and said, *"Momma, you just plug it in. That's all you have to do. I make a fresh pot for you every night."*

"I just plain forget."

"That's okay. We all forget things at times," Bernice

reassured her. And, only a few days later, her mother had become confused about how to use the oven to heat her dinner.

"She'll manage, I know. Momma's been through so much. I'll be glad when America grows up." Bernice cleared away the dishes and watched her mother sitting at the table.

How to Cope with Chronic Illness

The odds are that, as your parent ages, some chronic illness will develop. People over sixty-five, if they have not done so already, are at high risk to develop arthritis, emphysema, diabetes, cataracts, Parkinson's and Alzheimer's disease. When your parent is afflicted with a chronic, life-threatening illness, you want to do everything in your power to help; at times you may even wish *you* were the person with the disease rather than they.

The most common problem of persons over sixty-five years of age and one that causes more discomfort and loss of function than any other condition is osteoarthritis. The accompanying pain, tension, and anxiety leads to the development of chronic illness behavior, such as resisting the movement of joints. In turn, this immobility leads to muscle wasting and weakness, the result of which is diminished joint protection, increased pain, and a proneness to injury and falls. The cycle continues until the elderly shuns any activity and degeneration ensues.

You should be alert to the tricks and traps your parent may fall into. Try to help him/her take an active role in mastering the disease instead. Some of the most common traps are:

—feeling sorry for themselves;
—thinking they can't make it;
—becoming angry about the illness;
—wanting everyone to take care of them or wanting no one to care for them;
—feeling sad, lonely, and rejected.

While it is natural for these feelings to occur from time to time, chronic manifestation will certainly foster deterioration. The elder's sense of helplessness will increase, along with demands, and the impact of the illness on everyone will become more severe.

If you, as the adult child, fail to promote the parent's health and encourage proper medical and emotional management of the difficulties associated with the illness, you become, unwittingly, a problem for everyone. Conversely, by learning to properly support you can become the greatest helper. When a house is filled with promise and hope, seemingly insuperable problems can be overcome.

HELPFUL HINTS
- Set a positive tone. Encourage your parents to believe that they can cope with the illness and improve their health. Be firm.
- Follow the preventative treatment plan the health

care provider recommends. A sound medical plan includes:

—knowledge about the disease;

—workable pain relief methods;

—proper health habits: diet, personal hygiene, adequate rest;

—no narcotics dependence;

—no alcohol or tobacco;

—regular appointments with caregivers, as required;

—compliance with the medical plan;

—regular exercise, when appropriate.

- Avoid overprotection. A constant danger with a chronic disease is that the people closest to the patient assume a mode of behavior that promotes dependency. Both fall into the same trap. Therefore, learn to detect manipulation and stop participating in it.
- Encourage all family members to agree to work together to help the parent master the chronic illness.

A Walk to the Table

"You don't know how it hurts," Inez said as her son helped her to the walker for their daily trek to the dining room table for lunch.

"Yes, I know."

"But you can't; you're not walking," Inez insisted.

For the past six months she had complained more and more about walking because of worsening arthritis. Her knees were often swollen and sore, and this latest indignity had come despite her having walked all her life. The family had never owned a car, and she could not drive. Once she had called a horse and a buggy her own—a gift from her father when they lived on the farm. "I can make it only one way. Don't make me walk back, will you?"

Tom was aware of the discomfort, but he also knew that, once his mother gave up, her joints would only deteriorate further and the wheelchair would be her only means of mobility. She did better when she walked; her body was stronger. "Mother, I know it hurts, but if you don't walk a little each day, you'll just sit and rust away, and that's no good. Come on, we'll go as slowly as you need, but we'll get there. There's a big bowl of soup waiting for you."

"Okay, but only one way." They moved slowly. "Wait, wait, I can't get my feet to move." After first trying in vain to lift her right foot, Inez was slowly making her way over to the table. "Hold me; I don't want to fall!"

"I won't let you fall," her son reassured. The easy way out would have been to give in to her request to ride in her wheelchair, but there was too much at stake. "Mother, you did it! I knew you could," Tom praised, as they reached the table.

"I did; I used to love to walk. I wish my arthritis would go away. Some days I feel better than others. I know you're right. It's just that it hurts."

Special Problems for Aging Men

Just as their female counterparts, aging men are vulnerable to many chronic illnesses such as Parkinson's disease, emphysema, and arthritis. However, a few particular conditions affect only men: prostatism and prostate cancer and impotence. Both create medical as well as emotional problems but can be successfully treated in the early stages of development.

Prostatism

Your aging father has a one-out-of-three chance of developing an enlarged prostate gland after he reaches fifty years of age. Among older black males, the rate is much higher. This gland is located at the neck of the bladder, covering a part of the urethral canal through which urine is passed. Its function is to produce seminal fluid that carries the reproductive sperm. As it enlarges, the normal passage of urine is inhibited. The urine accumulates in the bladder and later backs up into the kidney where it causes damage and infections. Some men consider it as only a nuisance at first, but it should be taken seriously. Prostatism can cause disability and lead to serious illnesses if not treated properly.

Specific recognizable symptoms appear: frequent nighttime passage of urine, a limited amount of urine with little force in the stream of urine, painful episodes in trying to urinate, and the feeling that each urination is not complete.

The family doctor or a urologist can detect an enlarged prostate gland during an examination. If your father has developed prostatism, various treatments are available, such as removing the urine collected in the bladder by way of a rubber tube, and, if required, prostate surgery to remove a part of the gland to unblock the canal. Many elderly men respond well to this surgery.

Prostate cancer, the second leading type of cancer among black males, is a serious condition that can be successfully treated, especially if detected early. During examination, the evidence of cancer can be detected. The symptoms of prostate cancer are identical to those of prostatism. If detected, treatment should begin immediately.

HELPFUL HINTS

- Encourage your father to have an annual rectal examination to ensure early detection.
- Ask your father, if you feel comfortable, to let you know if he has trouble urinating. Many older men fear discussing urinary functions and may delay appropriate attention.
- Notice if your father goes to the bathroom frequently at night. If so, ask him to consider seeing a doctor for an examination.
- Discourage any use of advertised medical remedies that claim to shrink enlarged prostate glands. They do not work.
- Assure your father that this condition is common and can be treated effectively, especially when detected early.

They Don't Always Tell You

The son noticed the urine stains in his father's underwear as he did the laundry. When Mike took his eighty-year-old father places, he was aware that visits to the men's room were long and his father appeared exhausted. Finally, after a month of noticing the frequent trips to the bathroom each night, Mike asked his father about the problem and both agreed a visit to the doctor was necessary.

"I don't want to, but I will. I'm not going to be around much longer, anyway, son," the father said with his usual gloom. Never a person to anticipate joy, the old man always expected the worst.

"At least we'll know," Mike said as he made the appointment.

Two weeks later, prostate surgery was performed and no cancer was detected. Within a month, recovery was complete and Mike assured his seventy-six-year-old mother, "Dad's going to be fine until the next thing hits him."

"Your father always keeps things from us."

Impotence

While it is unlikely that your aging father will discuss impotency with you, you should know about this potential problem. You may want to share the information with your parents in a nonintrusive way.

For many years, most impotence was thought to originate from situational and deep-seated emotional problems. However, today's view is that fully three-quarters of the cases have a physical basis. Conditions such as diabetes, stroke, spinal cord injuries, and diseases of the heart and blood vessels can cause impotence. Excessive use of alcohol and certain medications can also lie at the heart of this problem. Your father needs to realize that something other than his emotional condition may be involved.

Adult children who have both parents living may be able to learn about their father's impotence from a frank discussion with their mother. Impotence is not an inevitable part of growing old as a widely held myth purports. On the contrary, most healthy men over seventy-five have sexual intercourse.

Even when the cause is physical, many men compound their impotence by fearing they are unable to perform. With today's advances in treatment, almost all cases of impotence can be treated once the cause is known. Your father should be encouraged to discuss the problem with his physician. If he is referred to a urologist who specializes in the treatment of impotence, a variety of successful treatments can be prescribed.

HELPFUL HINTS
- Learn the latest medical facts about impotence. Be prepared to discuss it if the occasion arises, either with your father or mother.
- Know the options available and encourage your parents to discuss the problem with the family physician.
- Help your father understand that he does not need to feel embarrassed or resigned to the condition. Help is available and generally successful. Also, assure him that impotence is not a natural consequence of aging.
- Urge your parents to explore Medicare coverage eligibility for this condition; coverage for diagnosis and treatment is usually available. Also, check your parent's supplemental insurance coverage.
- Become involved if your parents feel comfortable

83

about including you. They may not. Accept that decision.

Sleep Problems Are Common

More than one-half of the people over the age sixty-five who live at home and an even larger number of those in nursing homes experience sleep problems. Contrary to a widely held view, such problems are not a normal part of the aging process. Many healthy older people sleep well each night. Those who have Alzheimer's disease, arthritis, heart problems, and depression may find it difficult to sleep. Developing a regular pattern of sleep habits is essential.

The most common sleep problems are insomnia, obstructive sleep apnea (loud snoring and breathless lapses of a few seconds that can cause death), and involuntary body movements. If your parent experiences any of the above, contact a physician.

As your parents age, they are likely to take naps during the day, retire early, get up early, and take more sleeping pills than necessary or healthy. These changes in sleep habits can produce problems that are a nuisance and can worsen progressively.

HELPFUL HINTS
- Use sleeping pills only when prescribed by the physician. Misuse of over-the-counter remedies is common but produces dangerous side effects such as

withdrawal, memory impairment, anxiety, and depression.

- Encourage your parents to sleep on their side or stomach if obstructive sleep apnea is diagnosed.
- Encourage your parents to go to sleep and get up at the same time each day.
- Propose a period of exercise before bedtime to help prevent a restless night.
- Suggest avoiding alcohol or caffeine and drinking very little fluids in the evening, especially if the parent is incontinent.
- Seek medical attention if your parent experiences involuntary leg movements and unintentionally kicks while in bed.

Where Did It Go?

"I could sleep anywhere, anytime. Remember when you took me to see that movie Earthquake *and I slept through it?" Inez was sitting on her bed speaking of memories that filled her sleepless nights. What had been keeping her awake for some time now were cramps in her legs.*

"Let's talk with your doctor," her son suggested. Her fatigue and long naps during the day had not escaped him.

"I'm sure you get restless. I always marveled at your ability to sleep through almost anything."

"Not anymore." Inez shook her head. "I dread going to bed some nights."

"We'll ask the doctor."

Loss of Vision Limits Their World

When your parents begin to lose their eyesight, as so many do, their world shrinks. The process is especially painful for avid readers. Keep regular appointments to check vision and change prescription glasses as required. To help read small print, keep a magnifying glass nearby. The Library of Congress has an excellent program for those with vision loss, providing free cassette players and audio recordings of books and magazines to listen to.

Consider Cataract Surgery

With the technological advances achieved in cataract surgery, the patient takes smaller risks, recovers faster, has fewer infections, and enjoys better vision than just ten years ago. This surgery, in which the clouded lens of the eyes is removed, can be performed on an outpatient basis. Most patients now have good vision three to eight weeks after surgery, compared to three months with the old methods, which were also painful and dangerous. Many older people remember the ordeal associated with cataract surgery and still fear the operation. They have not forgotten hearing about prolonged convalescence in dark rooms, thick glasses, and infections from the stitches that were required then. Modern surgery uses ultrasound to break up the clouded lens, and debris is suctioned out through an incision less than half the length of that made in surgery a few years back.

Some loss of vision in aging people is greatly feared, and unfortunately, almost always experienced. Surgery may restore eyesight.

HELPFUL HINTS
- Observe your parents' vision and, if you notice they have trouble, arrange an appointment with their ophthalmologist to determine the status of the vision and the possible need for cataract surgery. Allay their anxiety about outdated procedures.
- Provide assistance to them if they undergo the modern surgery; they will require help during the healing period after the incision and the placement of an artificial lens.
- Encourage prevention:
  —Drugs including simple aspirin may help prevent or delay the development of a cataract.
  —Vitamins E and C may help reduce the risk of cataracts forming.
  —There may be a correlation between smoking and cataracts. Encourage cessation.
  —Exposure to the sun's ultraviolet light may increase risks; encourage parents to wear a brimmed hat and sunglasses when outdoors.
- Keep a magnifying glass handy for reading small print.
- Consider using the Talking Books program (Library of Congress).
- Purchase or borrow large-print editions of magazines and books.

Let's Wait

Her mind was set against it. After all, Gladys had told her the troubles she had had following cataract surgery fifteen years ago, and then there was Essie who got an infection and lost sight in one eye.

"No, I don't want to take the chance," Inez stated flatly.

"But the surgery is very different today. You know how the doctor explained. You don't even go to the hospital," her son urged.

"I know, but if I accidentally bend over, like Gladys did, I could ruin everything. Besides, I can see just fine in the distance. I can read with my magnifying glass."

Her son could see persuasion wasn't working.

"We have the appointment next Thursday. Once it's over, you'll be happy. You love to read, and now it's difficult and glasses can't help. The doctor says you have cataracts and surgery is the only answer."

Inez dug in. She tried to change the subject by turning the television set on.

"I can see that program just fine."

Two days before the scheduled surgery, Inez developed a cold. She knew that surgery was impossible as long as she had a cold.

"I'm glad I have this cold. He won't operate now. Let's put it off. I'm afraid. The risk is too great. I'll live with what I have."

Her son accepted the decision for the moment but knew he must try to get his mother to reconsider. Having her vision was like having a window to the garden and the joy of her books.

Impaired Hearing Frustrates

When your parents reach age fifty, they may begin to experience hearing loss and by age eighty most will have some type of hearing impairment. The decline is gradual, but after age fifty hearing ability diminishes each year, little by little. Twenty-nine out of every one hundred persons sixty-five of age or older have impaired hearing, and fully forty-three percent of all Americans with hearing impairment (17.4 million) are sixty-five years old or older. The causes are many: exposure to loud noises over time (usually in their occupation or residential area), infections, vascular incidents such as a stroke, excessive ear wax, head injuries, and age-related changes in the ear mechanisms. However, the impact is felt most acutely in social interaction and those with hearing loss often react in ways that compound the problem. They can become fearful, withdraw from others to avoid embarrassment, limit their participation in activities once enjoyable, and some become suspicious of others. They may even deny having a problem—both to others and to themselves. These actions can cause others to view them as stubborn, self-centered, and mixed-up—negative labels that hurt and further isolate them.

Knowing the common signs of hearing impairment is useful. Most adult children can learn them through everyday interactions. Inappropriate responses to questions, being asked to repeat constantly and to speak louder, lack of response in a conversation, inattention, frequent misunderstandings of a conversation, and straining to hear are common signs that hearing loss is occurring.

Because there are different types of hearing loss, your parents need to know the exact nature of their condition. Hearing loss can be treated in many cases: by flushing the ear canal to remove packed ear wax, surgery, a hearing aid, and special training such as learning to receive visual cues from lip movements (speech-reading). Hearing loss, unlike vision loss, often goes undetected or unnoticed because there are no visible signs such as eyeglasses, a cane, or a walker that denote other disabilities. Most persons with hearing loss can be helped. You need to learn how to assist with this potentially devastating condition.

HELPFUL HINTS
- Encourage your parents to see their doctor for an examination or referral to a hearing specialist if you notice common signs of hearing loss.
- Help your parent, if necessary, to learn about hearing aids if the medical specialist recommends the use of one. Most elderly persons with hearing impairment can benefit from using a hearing aid, but not all. Always have a comprehensive hearing examination before securing a hearing aid. Follow these suggestions:
  —Shop for it as you would any other item and obtain the one that provides comfort, conve-

nience, and quality of sound that suits.
—Buy the aid with only those features needed to enhance hearing.
—Take advantage of the free trial period.
—Learn how to use and care for the hearing aid.
—Have your parent attend a hearing aid orientation and join them in order to learn what the hearing aid can and cannot do to improve the impairment.

- Encourage your parent to ask others to repeat what they have said if the parent doesn't hear well, and to tell others that they have a hearing problem.

- Limit background noise such as televisions, stereos, and other appliances in the room while talking.

- Speak slightly louder than normal but not too loudly or in exaggerated speech because sound is easily distorted and the message will not be any clearer. For some, an increase in volume does not improve the quality of sound or make words clearer. Shouting at a person with a distortion of sound impairment does not help.

- Rephrase the idea in simple, short sentences if your parent does not understand the message.

- Speak at a close distance, no more than six feet but no closer than three feet, and face your parent.

- Arrange the seating in a room with chairs no more than six feet apart in order to enhance hearing.

- Do not shout in their ears; position yourself to allow them to see your lip movements, facial expressions, and body movements.

- Provide a telephone with an amplified receiver to enhance their hearing.
- Inform friends and acquaintances that your parent has a hearing loss and encourage them to follow the above suggestions.
- Be patient! The loss of hearing can be a painful, unintentional burden in conversations. Frequent misunderstandings are likely. Anger further complicates and frustrates everyone involved.
- Repeat what others say in a conversation if your parent does not understand them due to the hearing loss.
- Do not exclude your parent simply because their hearing is difficult. They need inclusion in order to lessen their isolation.
- Provide remote control devices that allow access to volume control on television and stereo sets.
- Encourage them to attend social and entertainment events that provide assisted hearing devices (many theaters now have them installed to aid hearing).

Hearing But Not Hearing

The sound of the television could be heard as Tom drove into the driveway and opened the garage door. He knew his mother was listening to the nightly news. As soon as he entered the house, Inez used the remote control to turn off the set.

"Tom, they just announced that Jimmy Carter has decided to quit as President."

Tom waited for a moment. He knew his mother often misunderstood the announcers. "They talk so fast," she said. He moved over to the couch where she sat and pulled a chair close to her. "That's hard to believe. Are you sure?"

"I think so," Inez responded uncertainly. "You know, I don't hear as well when it's damp. It's been raining all week. You listen to the next news. I hope it's not true."

They sat and talked for a while. Inez's hearing was getting worse. She went to an audiologist to have the wax removed from her ears and each time her hearing diminished, special drops were put in them in the evening.

"Be sure to tell your friends that I can't hear well. When they call, I get things mixed up and I know they think I'm dumb."

Tom remembered some of the garbled telephone messages Inez delivered. "I've told them, Mother. They don't think you're dumb. In fact, they think you'd make a great secretary."

"Not anymore. I don't want to embarrass you."

"You don't. I tell them to talk slowly and a little louder than normal."

"Remember, put some drops in my ears tonight." She paused and looked up. "I hope he didn't quit. I like Jimmy Carter."

Understand Medical Insurance Claims Forms

The array of medical claims forms to be completed and the payment schedules for each insurance policy confuses many elderly parents. While it is hard enough for anybody to keep up with constantly changing procedures and coverage of medical and other insurance, it is a particular challenge for the person whose memory and vision are deteriorating and whose likelihood of having to make use of insurance policies grows daily. When the need arises, filling out the appropriate form and submitting it to the right address is a tremendous challenge for the elderly. In some cases, it is only to find out that their particular medical condition is not covered or that the policy has lapsed, either because timely payment got overlooked or because the premium was simply no longer affordable. In any event, the inability to collect from an insurer can cause great financial and personal hardship. It also happens that, given the maze of insurance offered, overlapping or duplicating policies are often purchased.

Clearly, the adult child has to help the parent choose proper insurance coverage, terminate inappropriate policies, and submit claims. A good understanding of Medicare and Medicaid as well as private and supplemental health insurance is essential. There's no avoiding grappling with bureaucratic procedures.

HELPFUL HINTS

- Discuss with your parents the status of their medical insurance when they reach sixty-five. Most become eligible for Medicare at that age.
- Obtain supplemental health insurance because Medicare does not pay all medical costs. Supplemental health insurance is expensive, and you may

need to arrange a method of payment. The common term used today for this type of insurance is "Medigap."

- Review each policy periodically to note changes, revisions, and coverage if your parent agrees to let you examine them.

- Offer to assist in submitting claims or arrange for someone else to do it if they are unable to cope with the procedure. Since 1990, Medicare rules require the health care provider to submit the claims for payment to Medicare. However, the patient is responsible for submitting supplemental claims in order to collect authorized reimbursements.

- Develop a plan to cope with catastrophic health care costs since most policies do not cover long-term medical care.

An Angry Moment

"Horsefeathers, Mother!" For the second time that day Sara used her father's phrase. Only, this time it was accompanied by slamming the checkbook on the desk so hard that the slap drowned out the horse and left a shocked silence for the feathers to be heard around the world. Her father would have never allowed her to raise her voice against her mother, and both mother and daughter were aware of this fact.

To add to the unraveling of the order, Sara's mother refused to acknowledge that Sara was directing unmistakable anger at her, and she sat at her desk in mock concentration, moving bills into little piles and securing them with paper clips. Hers was not a conscious delaying action.

The fact that she might be called upon to relinquish her desk work, which she saw as the last thing her broken body could manage in the matter of holding her house together, was simply not going to occur to her. She could no longer move around the kitchen, so someone else had to do the cooking. She could no longer keep the house, so someone else had to do the cleaning. The gardening had been given up years ago, but then she rationalized that as man's work.

Sara's mother had had to ask for help getting out of the tub the previous week and hadn't taken a bath since. She was not only embarrassed by her nakedness but also frightened by her inability to maneuver the process. She had struggled until the water had become quite cold and her teeth were chattering when Sara answered her calls. Her short-term memory, eaten away by 90 years, would not release the sight of her own twisted body in the bathroom mirror.

"Who was that wraith in the funny shower cap anyway?" "Could this be the tennis player who had cooked for and entertained a house full of her husband's guests without lifting a finger?" "Was this the caregiver, the musician, the mother?" "Could this ignominy really be hers?" "What was happening to time?"

She would simply put it out of her mind. It hadn't ever really been a thought. She didn't have time to think about it, and she really didn't have to think about those checks she had to write, and she really didn't have to think about the miserable feeling that maybe her own daughter found her to be a burden. Surely it was time for dinner.

Sara, in order to justify her own confusion and rage, proceeded to give in further to the downward spiral of the moment. "Mother, how could you continue to say you mailed this insurance premium when I have it here before my eyes with its envelope and it is clear that you have not. Can't you see that this is no longer a matter of your saying so will make it so? This company holds your health insurance. Health insurance, Mother."

Sara was now bending over the desk so close to her mother that she fancied she could see her thin, wispy hair moving in response to her admonitions.

She was shaking now. "That's all we need! You break another hip, and we lose the house because you forgot to pay your insurance premium. That's all we need, Mother!"

Her mother didn't seem to notice Sara. She was wedging a thumbnail between the paper clip in order to secure a thick envelope marked with words that looked something like "House Bills."

"Okay, okay. Next week, after I get all this organized, you can take it over."

Had the dog not scratched at the back door at this moment, Sara would have proceeded to point out to her mother the reason she could so accurately predict her reply even to the phrase "next week."

"Oh, God," Sara said to herself as she moved toward the door, "I suppose Tippy has forgotten his health insurance, too," and a picture of the dog in a shower cap at the desk washed over her for an instant.

No one had told Sara life was going to be like this. She felt like writing some of those Dick and Jane books she had studied as a child.

"See the middle-aged woman shouting obscenities at the mother she loves. See the middle-aged woman's life disap-

pear. See what happens next week when the lovely daughter chops up her mother with an axe!" "My God, this has to be happening to someone else," Sara thought as she opened the door. "Get in the house, Tippy. We're going to apologize to Mother, give recognition to our foolishness, and I'm preparing our specialty tonight: 'Crow Under Glass.'"

Going to the Hospital

Few things are more traumatic for the elderly than a stay in the hospital. Many are sure they will never return to their homes, especially if the condition is very serious. While many older people with chronic illnesses have had extensive hospital experience, both inpatient and outpatient, each visit presents emotional stress on family members. And, in some cases, the hospital stay is followed by a convalescence period in a skilled nursing facility. These are not only expensive facilities, but the patient can feel very lonely, and the experience can further diminish an already failing health and spirit.

HELPFUL HINTS
- Keep a packet of papers filed and marked "Hospital." In it place all necessary information you will need at admission. Include:
  —information about physicians;
  —loved ones' names, addresses, and telephone contacts;
  —insurance carrier;

—Medicare number and card;
—supplemental insurance card and number;
—living will and durable power of attorney for health care;
—list of medications currently taken and dosages;
—list of allergic reactions to medications;
—social security number.

- Have parent remove all jewelry and other valuables and put them in a safe place.
- Learn the names of nurses in intensive care if your parent is placed there. Ask about the status of your parent and develop a positive relationship with hospital staff to ensure your visits are supportive.
- Be prepared to be persistent if your parent is in a large urban hospital. Many patients, especially elderly ones, are overlooked by busy medical staff. Ask necessary questions and remain calm.
- Keep your name and telephone number on the hospital bed's side table for easy access for your parent and medical staff to contact you.
- Consider obtaining the services of a nurse liaison, privately employed, if you are unable to visit your parent because of geographic distance. These services help you make decisions and provide support. They are expensive.
- Provide comfortable clothing for your parent. Sweatsuit materials are now used for gowns, robes, and slippers. They are comfortable, easy to launder, and inexpensive.
- Assure your parent that everything is taken care of

at their home while they are in the hospital and allay their fears of returning to an unkempt home.

Small Victories Soothe

This trip to the hospital was different from the last one when Ruth had a hip replacement. She had fallen and received a serious fracture. Ruth, a gentle compliant woman, had left the hospital stubborn and combative. The hospital staff called her a difficult patient. Medication for pain wrenched an already tenuous hold on reality. She saw bugs on the windows and she conversed with imaginary friends. Her son spent his days protecting her from the callousness found in large hospitals operated by underpaid and overworked staff.

Ruth recovered and returned home. As the pain medication was discontinued, her clarity slowly returned, but with it emerged a person her son did not recognize. His mother was suspicious and fearful of losing control. She needed assistance to walk. Her hair grew long and seemed dirty, and she was indifferent about her grooming. Before, she had been fastidious about her appearance.

At first bemused by her intransigence, the son soon became irritated and depressed. The matter of taking a shower instead of a bath became a week-long wrangle. In desperation, he called his mother's physician in her presence to confirm a Tuesday morning appointment. "We'll be there," he replied and hung up the telephone. "Mother, you have an appointment with Dr. Moss. He has forbidden you to use the bathtub because of your hip. I'll put the shower chair in place and help you sit on it. We can get the right water temperature. You want to be clean for your doctor, don't you?"

Ruth grumbled, but complied. He thought about this small victory—for both of them: his mother was clean again, and he was not as depressed. Aware of how solitary they had become, he took another chance.

"I tell you what, Mother, I'll call Louise. You haven't seen her in a long time, and we could meet for lunch after your appointment. We'll eat at your favorite cafeteria and order the food you and I like. Let's do it, okay?" He awaited a reply as he moved to pick up the telephone.

Ruth nodded acceptance. Small victories were all he was looking for, and it worked.

Managing Medication

One-third of prescriptions written today are for seniors and most use drugs on a regular basis; in fact, many take three or more drugs on a daily basis. For those who suffer from a chronic illness, medications help them sustain the quality of life. However, our parents may not know how to manage their use of medications, particularly as they become older and memory loss occurs.

HELPFUL HINTS
- Encourage your parent to do the following when they visit the doctor:
   —Write out the problem, how long it's been occurring, and when it started.

    —List all the drugs currently taken and which
      physician prescribed each.
    —List over-the-counter remedies.
    —List all allergies and poor reactions to specific
      drugs.
- Find out the following (if the doctor prescribes
  medication):
    —Why do you need it?
    —When do you take it?
    —How long do you need it?
    —Are there side effects?
    —Does it interfere with another drug you're taking?
    —Is there an approved generic substitute?
- Establish rules for taking the medication:
    —Follow directions on the label.
    —Keep medication in a cool, dry place.
    —Discard expired prescriptions.
    —Do not use alcohol while on medication.
    —Do not share prescription medications with
      friends.

Face Dying Together

Discussing dying is painful and frequently avoided in conversations between parents and children. However, being prepared and sharing decisions about these sensitive topics can put one at ease and may prevent unanticipated problems. Many children learn of their parents' deaths unaware of their wishes. Resulting family conflicts could have been avoided through facing death candidly.

As we all know, people are living longer these days due to improved medical technology. Often, the process of dying is long and arduous, and some hear their parents cry out for death.

While rare, the elderly can communicate suicidal intentions, and they have to be taken seriously, as many truly want to end their lives and are quite capable of taking action. Children must be alert to the following signals:

—expressions of sadness, defeat, and worthlessness;

—concern over a move from familiar surroundings;

—grief over the death of a spouse or child;

—suddenly putting personal affairs in order or giving away prized possessions;

—failure to take medications and abrupt changes in grooming and care;

—mood swings toward severe depression.

If your parent begins to signal any or several of these behaviors, take them seriously and help them obtain proper assistance.

HELPFUL HINTS
- Be alert to the effect newly prescribed medications have on elderly patients. Learn about potential side effects and inform the physician immediately. Med-

ications taken for the first time may cause depression, confusion, agitation, physical complications, and other undesirable conditions. The use of some tranquilizers increases the risk of hip fracture (more than 200,000 hip fractures occur in people over age sixty-five each year). Common side effects such as drowsiness, confusion, and impaired motor abilities increase the risk of falling. Check with your parent's physician if you suspect a tranquilizer is causing any of these problems.

- Discuss suicide directly with your parent and obtain assistance from professionals if you feel the problem is serious. Sometimes a long, reassuring talk can relieve the feelings that push people to take their own lives. Be alert to mood and behavior changes that signal an intent to commit suicide.

- Ask them if there are special things you can do to ensure that their wishes are carried out, such as to whom special personal effects should go and which persons should be informed by letter or telephone call.

- Find out if they have business that would need attending to such as canceling magazine subscriptions or club memberships.

- Take time today to tell your elderly parents that you love them and what they have meant to you, if your relationship with them is genuine and mutually positive. Many loving parents die without hearing this feeling expressed by their children. Find an appropriate time and, if you can, add humor. You may want to preface these remarks with, "We never know what's going to happen to either of us, so today I want to tell you how I feel. It's been on my mind a long time, and I want you to know . . ."

The Bed Is the Boat for the Spirit

"I know this will be hard on you, but I just want to die in my sleep. I want to go to bed and close my eyes." Inez sat on the couch with pillows supporting her back. Her feet were soaking in hot salt water.

"I've never heard you talk this way before." He was concerned. His mother had been ill for two weeks. She slept most of the time; her spirits were low. Even the lighted Christmas tree failed to bring cheer.

"Phil asked me many times how long did I want to live, and I always told him 'as long as I can be useful.' I never wanted to outlive my usefulness. I can't do anything for you anymore, and Phil's grown up and gone away."

"That's not true about not being useful anymore. You're wonderful company for me. I need someone to talk with and to share things when I come home. It's important to know you're here. You're always here. I can count on you," Tom reassured his mother.

"But I'm a burden now. I'm more trouble than good," she said. Inez was depressed.

Her health was remarkable. For the first time in five years, she had been to see her physician. The office visit three days earlier had tired her—she had taken tests for everything: a chest X-ray, an EKG, blood samples, and a urine specimen. She had an infection around her left ankle and had felt dizzy when she walked down the long hallway from her bedroom to the front room. With four new prescrip-

tions, she left the doctor's office late in November. Both mother and son harbored an unspoken dread as they returned to the home.

On the first day of December the Christmas tree was decorated and gifts were wrapped, fully two weeks ahead of the usual schedule. Inez loved the Christmas lights, and the sight of a brightly decorated tree prompted the characteristic yearly pronouncement, "That's the most beautiful tree I've ever seen."

"Mother, this is your ninety-ninth Christmas. We'll say it's your one hundredth next year."

"I don't know about that." She watched some of the strings of lights flash on and off. "I'm glad you put the tree up early this year."

"Phil will come home, and you'll be here to take care of him."

"All I can do now is talk," she replied sadly.

"That's enough."

"You know what to do when the time comes."

"Yes." Years earlier, plans had been discussed and agreed upon. Her ashes would be returned to the west Tennessee farm and a marker placed in the family graveyard, next to her mother's and father's monuments. A simple service would be held in the family church. The tall oak trees, the comfort of the red clay land, the corn and soybean patches, and warm, humid air in the summer would surround.

"I'd like to sleep now. Could you take me to my bed?"

"Yes, but you've been spending a lot of time in bed lately. That's not like you, Mother."

Her eyes were bright blue, the color intensified by a blue

106

sweater and a white shawl about her shoulders. "I guess I'm a little tired."

After the bed was prepared and she lay quietly under the blanket, her white hair against the two pillows, Tom stood looking at her for a long time. The bed is the boat for the spirit, a friend told him once. "You're born in a bed, you sleep, you make love, you nap, and in your dreams your thoughts leave your body as the mind travels to unanticipated places and people and things. And you may die in bed." Tom knew she lay there, wanting the latter, because she thought it was her time. She was ready. He wasn't. On Christmas day, they opened the gifts, laughed, and watched the fire burn until there were only embers.

When They Die

Our parents will die—some earlier and more painfully than others—but for each of them, death will be a unique unfolding and closing. While most of us will not be fully prepared for it, the time will come. To watch a parent die slowly over time compares with no other experience in our lives, and we cannot anticipate the impact. However, decisions can be made in advance that help us get through.

Parents dread the death of a child, and the agony is compounded when that child is their caregiver. Because people are living longer and many older children care for their parents, some will die before their parents do and a new decision about who will care for the parent must be made. Families with several children should plan accordingly.

HELPFUL HINTS

- Learn the type of funeral they want. Discuss your own funeral plans with them to ease the tension. Take care to check out prefuneral investments. Some unscrupulous persons in the funeral industry may try to take advantage of your grief.

- Encourage your parents to set aside a bank account with a child as cosignatory to pay for these expenses. Having access to money when needed can relieve financial and emotional strains that arise when funds are held up by probate. Stress to your parents that they are empowering themselves to be in charge at the end.

- Thank those who assist your grieving family. Many religious institutions and neighbors give comfort and sustenance during the time it's most needed.

- Give yourself and others time to reconcile the many emotions that will ensue.

Our House Has Many Mansions

Sara had imagined the call many times. She had dreaded it and looked forward to it all in the same moment. Now it was here. Sara heard her voice congratulating her brother on the job he had done over the years.

"She's gone." Two little words. "She's gone," he said. "I came into her room around six o'clock this morning and she had gone." He wept.

All the worry about how it would come to pass was over.

No hospitals, no tubes, no strangers hauling her from bed to chair. She had died in her sleep in her own bed—exactly as she said she wanted to go—exactly as her children prayed she would. Sara cried in sorrow and relief, cried in a tangle of emotions that wouldn't untangle for a long time.

Years ago when Sara's father died, her mother had been subjected to the classic funeral industry ripoff. In a state of grief, she had had to make all of the confusing decisions attendant to funerals. She determined with her children that nothing like this should ever happen to the family again. This time, the major decisions were already made. The funeral had been prepaid. All the hassles over open and closed casket, cremation or burial, and the final resting place had been concluded years before. So, when the family converged in this final ceremony, there were no decisions about how it should be done or who was in charge. It didn't matter to her children whether or not their own sensibilities were in accord with her decisions. Each in his own way saw the ceremony as a last gracious gesture of their mother. They could wrangle over their own matters not hers. Hers had been a long life, well-lived and the funeral carried an unmistakable undercurrent of celebration.

Her children, who in their earlier years had looked on their mother's connection with her church as something that old women "just did," were now the benefactors of the church women who saw to it that prepared food was brought to the house each day. During that time of confusion and grief, the refrigerator groaned with food. The church women brought their dishes and stayed just long

109

enough to let the children know they were there for them and that their mother was important to them. The children, not churchgoers, were at first embarrassed, and then impressed, and, finally, grateful at this organized show of devotion.

It had all gone so smoothly, no one wanted to think of the things that would not be covered by ceremony. When they were young and they called upon their mother to explain the conflicting complexities of life, she would sometimes reply, "Oh, my Father's house has many mansions." In grief, her daughter recognized that these mansions were infinite, and in each burned the fires of grief—fires which raged away, clearing the dimensionless interiors. Whether or not these fires would be put to rest would be decided moment to moment.

The morning following the funeral, Sara had already filled a Goodwill bag with old clothes that she herself could not wear. Her mother's medications had been thrown out. It was the shoes that did it. In the last few years of her life, her mother's feet had been so painful that the only footwear she could manage were sneakers, and toward the end, there was only one pair that she could get over her swollen feet and ankles. She was a proud, fastidious woman. The sight of her old misshapen sneakers with the shiny outline of her feet in their interior finally did its work. Sara sat on the floor of the closet and sobbed—for herself, for her brothers, and for the emptiness of her mother's sneakers. The trash bag could have the rest but not these. It would be several weeks before Sara could bring herself to throw them out. The fire raged, then died. She had survived.

The day she opened her mother's dresser drawers, the

smell of perfumed handkerchiefs ripped the doors right off one of these mansions. Sara's sorrow was so final and complete that, for a moment, she believed there would be nothing left of her. This experience would repeat itself unexpectedly over the months to come. She longed for just one more hour with her mother. Sara had heard people speak of the finality of death. Now she understood the heart of the word "final." All Sara wanted was just one more moment with her mother to tell her how great she had been, how much she missed her and loved her. Just one more moment to hang out. "Oh, it was all so clichéd."

She knew now why people ran off to tacky séances or to find their loved ones in butterflies and other reincarnations. "Of course," she thought, "who wouldn't wish the stone to be rolled away from the entrance." And in that instant, one of the recently gutted mansions was flooded with compassion, extinguishing the remaining embers of grief and making way for the whole new redecoration to come.

Consider a Living Will

Most people hope to die a quick, painless death when the time comes. However, we all have to reckon with the possibility of a life kept flickering only with the help of life support systems and/or advanced medical intervention. The right to select and demand the type of treatment or to refuse specific treatment is fundamental but often not taken. If slowly dying patients give up these rights or are not aware of them, they are kept alive, painfully at times, even though recovery is more than unlikely. They are particularly vulnerable to pain, indignity, and the enormous costs incurred by life-prolonging methods. Most would like to avoid this kind of a long drawn-out exit, and their children normally concur.

Forty states now recognize the Living Will, a document signed by the (would-be) patient, directing physicians and other care providers, family, and any surrogate to carry out his/her last wishes and abstain from unwarranted treatment. The will is executed when, under circumstances of physical or mental terminal incapacity, the patient cannot make decisions about medical care. The will allows the patient to exercise guidance and authority in these matters that must be adhered to.

Determining the wording of the will can provide an opportunity for children and their parents to discuss the critical issue of medical care during terminal illnesses. With Alzheimer's disease now affecting millions of older Americans, these family discussions are becoming ever more imperative. The Living Will should be drawn up while the parent is lucid and capable of expressing wishes and instructions. In most states, it is renewable at five-year intervals.

When a patient becomes permanently unconscious and no reasonable expectation for recovery exists, the patient can state that being kept alive by artificial means is unacceptable. All life-sustaining treatments such as tube-feeding, forced respiration, and resuscitation, and dialysis may also be rejected in advance as stated in the

Living Will. A surrogate authorized in the Living Will can execute the intent of this legal document.

HELPFUL HINTS

- Obtain information about a Living Will from your parent's physician or the county medical society.
- Learn the intent and implementation of the Living Will, if it is recognized in your state, and follow instructions for preparation and execution. Each state has different legislation and forms to be followed. Be sure you follow your state's requirements in order to assure its validity.
- Discuss the intent of the Living Will with your parents and, if they concur, encourage them to decide on the health care instructions to be given when there is no reasonable expectation of recovery from a serious or lethal illness or condition.
- Follow the specific steps required to ensure that the document is legally sound.
- Have the parent decide if, when death is inevitable, they wish to die at home or at the hospital, and state such instruction in the document.
- Give a copy of the Living Will to all family members, attending physicians, their lawyer, and the minister, if you wish.
- Give the Living Will to nursing home personnel if your parent is admitted or resides in one. Under the 1990 Patient Self-Determination Act, the patient has the right to accept or refuse medical treatment and to prepare advance directives (Living Will and Durable Power of Attorney). The law also

113

applies to hospitals, hospices, and other health care facilities that receive money from Medicare and Medicaid programs.

- Keep a copy of the Living Will in a safe, accessible place. Some carry a credit-card-size copy for quick retrieval.
- Review the Living Will at least every five years and initial and redate it to inform others that your wishes are current.
- Consider preparing your own Living Will when you help your parents write theirs. You can mutually discuss dying and death in a nonthreatening manner.

Select a Durable Power of Attorney for Health Care

In order to strengthen the directives presented in the Living Will, elderly parents can appoint someone to act as a health care agent to execute a durable health power of attorney. The stand-in appointed provides them with someone who can speak if they are in a coma or can no longer issue orders. It also allows the parent to describe their wishes for life-prolonging treatment or the lack thereof. This agent or attorney-in-fact is given the power to make health care decisions for the parent and must act consistently with their stated desires when that ability is lost.

Because the decision to designate a surrogate decision-maker is an important one, care must be taken to appoint a person who knows your parent's wishes and agrees with the intent stated in the Living Will.

The application of the Durable Power of Attorney for Health Care varies by state. Many do not recognize it at this time, and the procedures to establish and implement it vary. Assigning alternate agents is acceptable in some states but not in all. The agent is prohibited by law from authorizing anything illegal, acting contrary to your parent's known desires, and doing anything clearly contrary to your parent's best interests.

HELPFUL HINTS

- Discuss the role of the Durable Power of Attorney for Health Care with your parents. If agreed to, obtain the forms and instructions issued by your state. Each state has different legislation and forms. Be sure you follow their requirements.
- Study jointly the documents and descriptions of the plan and determine if your parent wants to proceed with the assignment of an attorney-in-fact to carry out the health care decisions made in the Living Will.
- Do not appoint a person who is a witness to their Living Will.
- Decide upon two alternate agents, if desirable.
- Discuss the role and actions of the health care agent with the designated person to ensure that your parent's wishes are understood.
- Review this document and complete it in accordance with the legal mandates of your state; other-

wise, it will be invalid. The document can be revoked at any time.

- Review the document periodically; some states have time limitations. Keep the document in a safe place and distribute copies to those who have received a copy of the Living Will.

Someone Give Me a Pill

"If I ever get like that, someone give me a pill." Over the years, it has been woven into the humor of the family. It was used to declare exasperation, "Oh, somebody give him a pill"; for an embarrassed apology, "Why didn't someone slip me a pill?" But no one ever carefully discussed its implication. Over the years, it became an assumed value shared by parents and children. Many professed to eschew living beyond their usefulness. Ruth always said, "I'd rather wear out than rust out."

Over the years, as Ruth grew frail, her criteria for usefulness changed. Her husband was gone. Many things once familiar were blurred. She seldom left the house. Her dogged concentration on what she could do saved her spirit. She could heat her coffee and toast her bread. Conversing with her friends and children by telephone gave her joy. Although she could write a check, she lost track of her finances.

"I'm just resting my eyes," Ruth said when her son asked if she was asleep. He noticed that she slept more than before.

Her last good friend had a breast removed at eighty-five. Having cancer at eighty-five was the ultimate betrayal.

Her friend was drained by radiation treatments. Her hair fell out, and she could hardly hear.

Ruth looked at her daughter, Sara, and said, "I don't want this for myself. Just give me a simple pill. Living death is not what life is about." She meant what she said. When the time came, she wanted it that way.

"But Mother," Sara replied, "you can do it another way. Have you heard of a Living Will?"

"Yes, somewhere, but not much."

Sara told her mother about the Living Will and the Durable Power of Attorney.

"What do you think of that?" Sara inquired, as she watched her mother lean against the walker and rest her head on the top bars.

"I want to die naturally—no artificial life for me. When it's my turn, I want to go. Don't put any tubes in me. Don't fill my lungs with oxygen. Don't keep me hanging on in a coma. Promise me, Sara, that you will do that. Are you sure we can?"

"Yes, Mother, we'll get the papers and talk about it. I already have one for myself. We'll start right away."

"Good! At least I may have the right to die the way I want to. I don't want a fancy machine to keep me alive. Just give me a pill."

CHAPTER 4

------- ◆ -------

Enriching the Final Years

As parents age, their lives can be marked by the things they can no longer accomplish. On top of their health concerns, they may lose friends (to death or relocation), interests that once sustained them, the ability to travel and communicate, familiar surroundings, and their sense of self. Unless creative responses are forthcoming, particularly from their family, such losses can be devastating.

Aging is often synonymous with losing old ways of doing things, and these changes are disconcerting. In fact, if you notice your parents' actions over time, as pointed out earlier, the one constant is their shrinking world. Some parents give up things more quickly than others, but the certainty is that one by one old routines,

119

interests, and activities disappear, sometimes unnoticed by others or even by the parents themselves. As they discard the once familiar, their children should become alert to these voids and find ways to enrich their lives.

Social Isolation

Social isolation comes in various forms:

- Immediate family members are deceased or live far away.
- A residential facility allows limited contact from the outside.
- They are alone in their own home or apartment, afraid of surroundings.
- Physical and/or emotional disabilities thwart close and loving contacts.

The fear of being alone or rejected and neglected comes to haunt many of our older citizens. Those who have living children but are ignored by them suffer the most, perhaps because they must learn to cope with the loss of once familiar social ties and a feeling of betrayal. Adult children can do many things to enhance social contacts. One of the cruelest circumstances of the final years is the isolation of caregivers and parents. Slipping into routines without contact with others can hasten the sense of remoteness and despair. And losing once close friends because of the new living arrangements with constant demands and little time for other than the routine hurts.

HELPFUL HINTS

- Be alert to the time elderly parents can no longer travel unassisted for long trips. They may let you know, but if they don't, you should intervene if you note a potential problem. Calmly point out that the trip will be too taxing—physically and emotionally.
- Encourage the parent to maintain other types of contact with relatives and friends, such as regular correspondence, telephone calls, and exchange of gifts, cards, and photographs on special occasions. Establish set times for regular phone calls from relatives, if possible.
- Discuss the past and reassure the parent that memories are important. Look at old photographs and newspaper clippings together and read over old letters. If you have a grandchild in the family, these activities can be particularly rewarding to them.
- Invite relatives and friends to visit the parent in order to maintain personal contacts and to assure the parent that others care. Having visitors encourages parents to dress up and keep up with current developments.
- Celebrate special occasions, such as a birthday. Many older Americans have not celebrated a birthday for years. Invite friends and relatives, if possible.
- Encourage relatives and friends to write letters that require an answer from the elderly parent.
- Utilize church, synagogue, and other appropriate

community services for additional companionship if the elderly parent is interested. Elder day care programs are often stimulating. Group tours and day trips arranged by senior centers provide stimulation.

- Do not withhold information about the family from an elderly parent, unless you determine that the news would definitely upset them. Elderly parents, like all other members, need to feel a part of family affairs, both the good and the bad.

A Big Pot in a Little Pot

As time went on, Inez Adams did not return to open her Tennessee home for the summer. At age ninety-four, she discontinued her yearly trek to open the family house, invite the children, grandchildren, and great-grandchildren to share a vacation. While there, she had cooked, washed, visited, and renewed contact with family, neighbors, and her four sisters-in-law. Summer in Tennessee was important because she was in her home, independent and self-sufficient. She didn't drive a car, had neither washing machine nor air-conditioning, but the house she and the family had lived in since the close of World War II was a most precious material possession, filled with memories. She had loved the house since she first saw it in 1920. They bought it in 1945 for $3500, making the final payment in 1956. House payments were $26 a month, including insurance.

"Inez, I never thought we'd own our home," her husband, Wiley, often said with pride. Her small farm in west Tennessee was important to her, but this house symbolized *their victory over the ravages of the Great Depression and the War. Her last summer there was filled with joy and apprehension. She knew the time had come to abandon the ritual journey. She would never see her home again. "It's like losing a dear friend," she wrote to her sister-in-law Gusta.*

"Inez, if you and Tom will come back this summer, I'll put a big pot in a little pot. You can stay with me. We want to see you again. We miss you so much." The weekly letter arrived in May, just before Inez's ninety-ninth birthday. She read it slowly and knew the reply.

"What does that mean—to put a big pot in a little pot?" Tom asked. He was intrigued by the expressions Aunt Gusta's letter contained.

"She'll do the impossible if we come. She'll make magic." Shaking her head, Inez smiled. "And Gus would. She always does. I wish we could go—but we can't."

Encourage Grandparents to Be Active

As parents age, few roles can be more joyful and useful than grandparenting. With the modern family likely to disintegrate at any time and with fully one in four families headed by a single parent, the need for grandparents increases each year. They are becoming the glue that holds many families together: families that are torn apart by divorce, financial stresses, unemployment, illness, and death. Grandparents bring unique contributions to happy as well as troubled families. They can offer a link to the past, unconditional love and affection to their grandchildren, and stability when other relationships and events are volatile. But adult children don't need to wait for a crisis to encourage their parents to become active grandparents. Let them know you need them and want them now.

Not all grandparents can become active. There are constraints such as living a long distance from their grandchildren; they may work; illnesses debilitate; past child-parent relationships may have been traumatic; differences in the way each disciplines a child may separate them; and they may feel like intruders. In spite of these constraints, try to develop a strong bond with your parents and grandparents.

HELPFUL HINTS
- Make a mutual agreement if necessary that discipline will be the prerogative of you, the parents.
- Find useful roles for grandparents: child care, recreation, reading, helping with homework, and other nurturing activities.
- Use holidays and summer vacations to convene the family for recreation and good times.
- Encourage aging parents to share their heritage with their grandchildren through visits, talking, letters, and phone calls.
- Involve grandparents in some decisions that affect the entire family—decisions about college, a career, travel, employment, school activities. Their knowledge can be used to reach important agreements and decisions.

- Include your parents in some aspects of childrearing if family needs warrant and they agree.
- Encourage your children to respect and appreciate the special wisdom and affection grandparents can impart.
- Encourage your parents to make the gifts they give grandchildren themselves if they have special hobbies and talents.
- Discourage expensive gift giving, especially when grandchildren are young.

I'll Find a Way

"My hand is really swollen," Phil said, displaying his right hand to his grandmother. He'd gotten oleander bush splinters in his fingers two nights before when he lost control of his bicycle and crashed into the large poisonous bush.

"That does look bad. I'll call the doctor." Inez examined the hand and thought about their being alone because Phil's dad was on a trip and would not return until the next day. She called the family physician only to learn that a doctors' strike was on.

"What will we do?" Phil pleaded. He had a music job on the weekend, playing his accordion at a party. At the age of twelve, he appeared regularly at parties and other special events. "Let's walk to town and find a doctor who'll treat me," he suggested. The eighty-four-year-old grandmother and the twelve-year-old boy walked from office to office and received the same response everywhere: The doctor is on strike.

Inez took care of her grandson and the house while her son worked and traveled. She worried that the condition of his hand would worsen. Her responsibility was to care for Phil, and she did all she could for him. Their concern grew each time they encountered another rejection. Phil wanted to call his father.

"But, Phil, we've got to find someone to care for you now," his grandmother insisted. At the next office, Inez demanded that someone see Phil. The receptionist gave her the name of a physician who was not striking. They walked to his office, tired, afraid, and alarmed. The fingers were swollen and painful.

"You got here just in time. That middle finger joint could be damaged. He should have X-rays. If the boy doesn't have these splinters removed, he could lose the use of his joints."

Phil looked at his grandmother. "That would end my music."

"What can we do?" Inez asked the doctor.

The doctor told her to get him to a hospital emergency room. Inez did not drive a car. The two looked at each other. She asked if he could do anything. The doctor put some medication on the finger and wrapped it. He suggested aspirin for the pain. As they left the office, Inez said, "I'll get you there. Don't worry, Phil." She knew they would find a way. They walked to a phone booth. She called the hospital emergency room. Yes, they would look at the finger. Doctors were on duty to treat emergencies. Next, she called a taxi, and they were soon on their way.

"Grandmother, I don't want to lose my finger."

"They'll help," she comforted.

Phil rested his head on her shoulder as they rode along the highway.

Retirement That Doesn't Work

Not everyone who retires finds leisure life satisfactory. Because they cannot make ends meet on their Social Security or pensions, they feel financially strapped and fearful of losing their lifelong possessions. Others may find that social isolation and lack of stimulation propel them toward returning to the work force rather than to engage in volunteer and recreational pursuits. They may miss the stimulation of the workplace.

In the early part of this century, most men worked until past sixty-five but today the majority of men and women retire at age sixty-two. With extended life expectancy, they have many years ahead of them. An increasing number are opting to return to work or seek a second or third career.

This return of the older person to the work force is being encouraged by many companies that find the older worker the more reliable one. With a shrinking skilled work force, job opportunities are increasing for retired persons. Your parents may want to consider a new career if they are in good health, need additional financial resources, or desire the companionship of colleagues and stimulation of a job.

HELPFUL HINTS
- Discuss the option of returning to the workplace with your parents if conditions are right.

- Balance their needs with their current situation. Discuss why this option could be a positive development.
- Learn about employment resources available in the community and contact those agencies that now provide services such as job finding and counseling for the older worker. The Area Council on Aging is a good place to start.
- Assist your parents, if they want help, to make the necessary arrangements for transportation, look into tax advantages, consider career training, and establish home security.

Capacities Do Diminish

Reduced capabilities of older people to cook, clean house, work on cars or in the garage, or shop, do laundry, and work in the garden become affronts to their self-reliance and self-esteem and require creative responses. Children can help by first becoming aware of the changes and then discussing how to fill the void. Parents may deny that things are different, and it will require patience on your part to help your parent move to another phase of life. Keep daily life stimulating!

HELPFUL HINTS
- Make or purchase an apron with several pockets, such as those used by carpenters, and encourage the parent to wear it during work times. Pockets can

hold dust cloths, tissue paper, scissors, glasses, a magnifying glass, a pen and tablet, the TV remote control, and keys, for example. Forgetful parents might otherwise spend time looking for these items. Having them readily at hand reduces the frustration and facilitates their work.

- Place several small watering cans near house plants to make watering easy. A large watering can may be too heavy to carry about the house, especially if the parent uses a walker or is otherwise frail.

- Encourage compiling a shopping list of family needs. By tracking these needs, the parent feels included and has the opportunity to assert food preferences.

- Place colored or textured tape or decals on oven, stove, microwave, washer, and dryer controls to identify appropriate temperatures or timing required for cooking and laundry. These markers enable people with poor vision and/or memory to prolong their involvement in household chores.

- Build a ramp at an exit door to facilitate mobility. Many elderly persons cannot walk down steps. The ramp allows those in wheelchairs access to the outside.

- Place rubber mats in the laundry room, kitchen, and bathroom if the elderly parent is able to cook, wash dishes and clothes, and take a bath alone. These mats provide cushions for feet and back and can keep the parent from tiring too easily. The mats also serve as cushions to break an unexpected fall.

- Keep a routine to avoid problems caused by unfamiliar circumstances. Help parents develop a way of doing things, such as how to get from the bedroom to the bathroom at night without falling or bumping into objects. Do not change their habits if they are content with a routine that enables independence.

- Install metal railings on the wall from bath to bed. Also install rails on the side of the bath for safe entrance and exit.

The Cabinet Drawers Are Closed

When Inez was ninety-seven, she became less able to keep her balance. As her fear of falling had recently increased, she left an unmistakable trail in the kitchen—a trail of fully opened cabinet drawers to which she secured herself as she moved about. While she was still able to bathe herself in the bathroom, she likewise opened drawers for bracing her short frame as she washed.

"Mother, you've been in the kitchen," her son noted one day.

"How did you know?"

"The drawers are opened," he laughed.

"I open them one by one to hang onto. I always feel safer," she said. Closing them was not possible because her balance would be jarred. Once she fell to her knees in front of the refrigerator and was sore for days. Having something to hold onto was what she needed, and the cabinet drawers were just the right height.

In the fall of her ninety-eighth year, Inez could no longer walk without assistance from a walker and her son beside her to prevent a fall. The kitchen returned to its normal appearance. She gave up her walking cane, preparing her meals, and washing the dishes. She also gave up open drawers, but a tidy kitchen is a poor bargain for that loss of independence.

For Inez, drawers were always places to save things. Once while she was away in Tennessee on her traditional summer trek to the family home, her son found mountains of used Kleenex and paper towels wadded in tiny balls and stuffed in the dresser drawers in her room. She saved them to ensure a ready tissue for her often running nose. During the day she thrust them up the sleeves of her dresses or sweaters, and at nighttime she deposited them in the drawers. When her gloves were missing, we looked up her sleeves and always found them. The collection of old tissues ended when she became unable to walk unassisted. The drawers no longer hold used Kleenex, paper towels, and old letters.

As their circle of friends and family tightens, as they lose lifelong friends and other family members, seniors need new roles and interests. Loneliness and apathy can be unbearable. Christmas card lists shorten. Regular correspondents vanish.

Art Saves Lives

Maintaining an active, positive outlook is important in preventing an older parent from slipping into boredom or depression, accompanied by a sense of uselessness.

Diminished capacities mean losing the talents, interests, and skills that once anchored them to familiar surroundings. It also means losing a positive spirit. At this point in their lives, humor and the ability to have some avenue for self-expression become life-savers.

HELPFUL HINTS
- Discuss your parents' interests and remember the things they liked to do as you grew up. They may have played a musical instrument, knitted, built, gardened, or painted. They may always have had a love for letter writing, dancing, singing, storytelling, and gossiping. Encourage them to continue.
- Make sure elderly parents have the necessary supplies to pursue their hobbies or interests.
- Discover ways to distribute the products they made or are still making. Find a home for that potholder or that tea cozy. They make nice gifts for family and friends or they can be sold in yard sales or in craft shops catering to items produced by seniors.
- Plan and maintain a working place for the elderly and arrange for them to attend elder care programs, if they are available in the community.
- Encourage them to tape record—audio and/or visual—messages and descriptions about their interests and talents to pass on to future generations.

Will It Be Mozart or a Polka?
"I think I'm going in and pound on the piano," Ruth declared, pushing back from the dining room table and

slowly lifting her frail hands to maneuver the walker. Gripping the rattling aluminum supports, her hands guided her toward the piano in the parlor.

"I'm so rusty, they should actually forbid me from touching the keys any longer; I make a terrible racket," she whispered as she sat down on the bench and shuffled through the sheet music.

Standing by the window, her daughter listened to the music floating through the house. It was awkwardly played, yet familiar and enduring.

"I'm glad we kept the piano, Mother. I remember that piece. Keep playing."

She remembered how her mother had played Mozart for herself, Bach for the church, and ragtime for parties.

Ruth bent over the piano, proud to be able to play at ninety. She often said that the flesh may be weak, but the treble clef would prevail.

Find Security and Comfort

Someone very aptly called the place in the home where a person finds regular security and comfort a "perch." For some it's the wheelchair in a nursing home where they may sit with a long line of others and stare into unfamiliar faces or into a vacant distance. For others, it's the bed that confines them to hold their sick, often twisted, bodies. For a few, it's the park bench or the doorway stoop. For the lucky ones, it's a favorite, over-stuffed chair or the desk in the den. Old people find their perch. It can be hard and cold and defeating—an unwelcome prison for the body and mind that exacerbates their vulnerability. But it doesn't have to be that way.

When the time comes, and it surely will for most, the perch can be made safe, warm, secure, and beautiful—a natural resting place that keeps life familiar, functional, and worthwhile. A true perch cannot be encroached upon because it belongs solely to its inhabitant.

HELPFUL HINTS

- Identify the perch your parent chooses—consciously or unconsciously—and respect its inviolability.
- Make it comfortable, if your parent wishes, with pillows, blankets, a footstool, and plastic protection if the person is incontinent.
- Provide a view to the outdoors, warmth during cold weather, light for reading, ample areas to perform tasks, flowers and house plants, and quiet when desired.
- Avoid encouraging the choice of an isolated area where the parent might feel exiled and alone—a back room or a hallway.
- Supply a TV remote device, magnifying glass, dark glasses to wear if bright light offends the eyes, a letter opener, pen and paper, magazines, newspapers, and other items a parent might use to help occupy the time and execute tasks. Note the kinds of things they are interested in and keep them at the perch.

- Make the telephone accessible (a cordless phone, an extension wire, and a nearby jack). If the parent's hearing is impaired, install an amplified receiver. If sight is impaired, use a telephone with extra large push buttons. By having the telephone easily accessible, an immobile person can be reassured and encouraged to communicate with others.

- Consider installing a speaker telephone for those who wish to use an amplified system that does not require holding the receiver.

- Make a list of the most frequently used telephone numbers and consider using a memory system that will enable the parent to place telephone calls easily with simple access.

- Discuss acquiring a companion animal, if the family has none, and make the choice consensual.

- Place a table or tray in the perch area to enable the parent to write and enjoy a meal or snack, and also to hold useful items.

- Provide large-type editions of magazines and books for those with impaired vision.

- Encourage exercises that strengthen muscles in legs, arms and hands. Soaking feet in warm salt water relaxes and helps cure foot ailments.

- Help keep the perch clean and neat.

The Perch

Two worn footpaths across the carpet identify the routes Inez has taken: one from her bedroom to the couch in the living room; the other from the couch to the kitchen and back. The two paths converge at the end of the couch, a green velvet-upholstered Empire antique restored by her late husband, Wiley, more than fifty years ago, when they lived in Tennessee.

"That's your mother's perch," the carpet cleaner commented one day as he steamed the soiled area beneath the couch. "People have a way of settling into special places. I find them in every home. This here is your mother's perch." He sprayed extra cleaning fluid on the area that was discolored by urine, dirt from shoes, and coffee.

Perch is an apt description. When Inez joined her son in California, she naturally settled at the end of the couch, and this spot has been her daytime base of operation for eighteen years.

"It's a thirty-minute couch. The seat is firm and the back is stiff and upright," she told her friend Edith. "Most can't sit here more than half an hour. My son says St. Paul probably designed it," she joked.

The long couch, made from crotch mahogany wood, was purchased in 1947 for twenty-five dollars. Wiley brought the pieces in burlap bags to his shop and carefully reassembled the fine antique that today could command a price of several thousand dollars.

Two large pillows, covered with plastic, render the seat comfortable, and two smaller pillows are used to soften the rigid back. Inez sits here for hours.

The tracks from the bedroom to the couch and to and from the kitchen were made unassisted, until a fall forced Inez to use a cane. When she became unable to keep her balance, she added a second cane and, with one in each hand, maneuvered with balance and safety until a second

*fall prompted the use of a metal walker. The more she had
to restrict her movements about the house, the more frequently the perch was used. Finally, at age 98, Inez
purchased a travel chair and quickly discontinued walking down the long path from her bedroom. To travel the
shorter distance from the couch to the dining room table,
where she has her meals, she uses a walker.*

*Inez's perch has become a command post, a self-
contained recreation center, and a secure spot in a changing world. A coffee table directly in front of her and a
rosewood cabinet table at her right are her demarcation
points. From the couch Inez operates the television with a
remote control device. Out the three large windows across
the room, she can see the front yard, a weeping willow tree,
the sidewalk to the porch, and the sky. While she can no
longer move among it, the view provides a connection to
life outside the house.*

"The postman is across the street at Mrs. Johnson's."

"I'll use my sunglasses; the sun is bright today."

*"Those joggers are wearing sweaters—it must be colder
today."*

"A man left a note on the door."

"The willow tree has new leaves."

*"The little neighbor boy found his cat on the porch
today."*

*"I saw your truck turn into the driveway. I'm glad
you're home."*

*"A wren is building a nest in the porch rafters. I
watched her come and go. I can't hear her sing unless the
front door is opened."*

Having tasks to fill the day breaks the lull, and Inez fills her day with activities that amuse, occupy, nourish, and make her feel useful. Some essentials surround: headlines in the mornings newspaper are read with a magnifying glass. Cataracts blur her near vision, but seeing afar remains a joy. Inez has no trouble seeing the small wind-mill twirl in Mrs. Johnson's yard, a full forty yards away.

During the summer, a vase of cut flowers from the garden adds warmth and color. Roses are Inez's favorite. During the fall and winter months, chrysanthemums and daisies occupy the vase on the rosewood table.

The couch serves as a work area. Inez folds the cloth diapers used as pads to cope with incontinence. She washed and dried them herself until a year ago, when she unwillingly abandoned that duty. "At least I can still fold them," she says each day as she arranges them in sets of threes and places them on the coffee table, pushing them into neat rows with her walking stick. Inez refuses to use disposable diapers.

At precisely 8:30 each Sunday morning, Inez receives a long-distance telephone call from her daughter in Chatta-nooga. A long extension cord allows the phone to be brought to the perch. Inez soaks her feet in hot water in a pan placed on the heavy throw rug. The rug is soft and warm. During the day, she rests her feet on a footstool to increase the blood circulation in them. She covers her knees with a wool blanket for warmth.

Companions on the couch are her choice of magazines—the recent large-print edition of Reader's Digest, *a Na-tional Geographic, and Newsweek. While fine-print text is too hard to read, headlines, combined with photo-graphs, convey meaning.*

A lamp on the rosewood table provides light when needed, and a wristwatch lies face up to help keep track of time. A cup of tea and cookies are within reach, and the rosewood table is also where her letters go after being read.

On television, Inez watches CNN *news, Tom Brokaw, talk shows,* As the World Turns, *Oakland A's baseball games, and the San Francisco 49ers football games. Movie classics round out her choices, and, with the volume turned up, the house could easily be mistaken for a teenagers' rowdy hangout.*

During the early 1980s, Inez's grandson told his friends to let the phone ring a long time because "it takes Grandmother five rings just to get up from the couch to begin the walk to the telephone." She efficiently took messages and conversed with callers who managed to understand her southern accent. Today, the telephone is brought to her.

When a fire burns in the grate, Inez remembers the long Tennessee winters. "I love to watch a fire burn. Mammy made fires with oak logs from the forest when I lived with her on the farm." Every Christmas season, Inez gazes at the tall Christmas tree with flashing lights and says, "That's the most beautiful tree I've ever seen, don't you think?" A fire roars in the grate, a soft rain falls against the large windows, leaves flutter from the weeping willow tree, and multicolored lights flash on the Christmas tree.

Pepe, the family's Siamese cat, shared Inez's perch for fourteen years. He would lie beside her and sleep, moving only if he saw a dog or cat intrude upon his front yard or porch. As companions, Inez and Pepe accepted each other. When Pepe died, Inez announced, "No one can take Pepe's

139

place. Let's not get another cat. I'm not able to take care of one anymore." Her plea was accepted.

Receiving mail has always been important to Inez, but, over the years, her correspondence has dwindled as old friends passed away. When she was mobile, she walked from the perch to the mailbox at the front door to retrieve the mail. As her fears of falling increased, she asked that a larger mailbox be installed and placed directly by the door. "I'm afraid I'll fall when I reach into that tiny box to get the mail. They cram so much junk mail in there." Her request was granted, and she made her way across the room, took the mail from the new, large box, and sorted it in stacks on the table. Today, she waits for the letters to be brought to the perch, and if they are written on colored stationery, she asks that they be read to her. "I just cannot read when the paper is blue."

Daily exercises are performed that help keep body and mind fit. Inez moves her legs up and down, bends her knees, and exercises her ankles. "Ernie said that if I exercise my fingers, that helps my arthritis," Inez explains as she moves the joints of each finger, curls her fingers, and counts as if she were playing the scales on a piano. "This makes my fingers nimble," she boasts.

"Do you always count as you exercise your fingers?"

"Not always. Sometimes, I just repeat words. I just say what's running through my mind. I have plenty of time to think."

Beside one of the large windows, a platform rocker sits directly across from the couch. It is another perch—from an earlier day. "Wiley sat in that chair when he got sick and couldn't work those last two years before he died. That chair was the only place in the house he'd sit. Once he sat in it for two weeks without getting up. I'd push it around like a wheelchair—it has glass rollers. I'd push him to the bathroom. That chair was all he wanted. There he'd eat, change his clothes, take a sponge bath, even shave once in a while. He'd ask for his razor, the strap, hot water, and his shaving mug. I'd say, Wiley, don't you think you ought to go to bed? He'd just say he wanted to rest—that he was tired. I thought he'd die in his chair. When I look at that chair, I remember our life in Tennessee. During one's lifetime, things have a way of repeating and coming full circle."

When darkness falls each evening, Inez asks that the drapes be drawn and says, "I'm afraid to sit in here alone with a light on. If anyone comes to the door and knocks, they'll see me alone if you're not here. I don't mind sitting in the dark for a while if you're a little late getting home tonight."

Grooming Can Brighten the Spirits

A good self-concept is enhanced by personal appearance, cleanliness, and grooming. Elderly people need to present themselves well in spite of obstacles created by ill health and diminished capacity. One of the greatest gifts one can give to another is to enhance a sense of well-being. A child can help the parent maintain dignity in appearance and ensure that proper clothing is available. What an elderly person wears can affect physical health as well as the spirit.

HELPFUL HINTS

- Find ways of helping the parent maintain a role in decisions about what to wear.
- Encourage the parent to select items from mail order catalogues if personal shopping is no longer an option.
- Provide loose-fitting clothing because the elderly need room to move about. Tight clothing and undergarments cut off blood circulation, and synthetic fibers can cut the skin and may be a fire hazard. Since many elderly sit for long hours, clothing should be simple, of natural fiber, easy to remove, and easy to wash. Full zippers in the back are preferable to buttons. Loose-fitting pants are good.
- Provide short, warm nightgowns, especially if the elderly are incontinent.
- Have warm sweaters, scarfs, and blankets for those who chill easily. When temperatures are changeable, the elderly can wear layers of clothing. Stockings and soft shoes provide comfort for those who sit for hours.
- Encourage short hair that is manageable and involve the elderly in hair grooming.
- Suggest white cotton stretch gloves for those whose skin is dry and itchy. The gloves reduce the danger of infection and protect the skin from abrasions made by fingernails. Gloves also keep hands warm.
- Make available the jewelry a parent desires. Some items may have sentimental value and enhance their appearance.

Last Year's Bird's Nest

Bernice had asked her mother about going out to shop now that the winter had passed and Dallas was basking in spring sunshine. Virginia was not interested and hadn't been for the past two years. Going window shopping together had once been a favorite pastime. When walking became difficult, they took the car and drove slowly by the stores in the mall and peered at clothing. Getting out was difficult.

Last winter was colder than usual, and they decided to forego the yearly trip to see the Christmas decorations on the old pecan tree across town. Later, Bernice thought a warm spring day might convince her mother to try getting out anyway.

"The windows at Harris's are filled with new things. Let's go. Remember when you said, 'I can't wear last year's bird's nest?' Let's get out today. Every molting bird needs new feathers," Bernice encouraged her mother.

"No," Virginia said. "Maybe next time."

Bernice realized her mother had rejected the same offer for two years.

"Well, okay," Bernice conceded reluctantly, painfully aware that her mother was forsaking a ritual they had enjoyed for years.

Bernice was unwilling to give up completely; she went to Harris's Department Store the following weekend and bought three of everything she thought her mother might want: three blouses, skirts, and sweaters. Change is often easier for an older person when it's shared, and so Bernice bought three blouses for herself as well, even though she didn't need them.

143

"Look, Mother," Bernice exclaimed excitedly as she spread the garments out for inspection, "new feathers for both of us."

Virginia was dismayed. "We can't keep all of them."

"I know, but I'll pick out the one I like best and I'll return the other ones. You do the same."

Bernice realized she'd come upon a way to give her mother a say in what she wore, and they continue to shop in this fashion today; Bernice brings three items, and her mother selects the favorite. Window shopping is now closer to home.

A Spiritual Bond to the Past

A common tie among the elderly is their religion, especially their religious ties to the past because their generation lived during the period in which these institutions were foremost in their lives. As they age, their access to them changes but their spiritual and ritual connection may not fade.

Through television, some of the larger dominations buy air time to minister to those who cannot enjoy the personal fellowship of their friends and fellow worshippers. Many older people use the media as a way to remain connected to their religious roots. In recent years, some television evangelists have used their charisma for personal gain and wealth. However, many religious services aired on television provide a proper spiritual experience.

Those with significant ritual such as the Catholic Church send eucharistic ministers (lay people instructed in the ritual) to serve communion to elderly members who are homebound.

Many churches and synagogues organize groups to regularly visit those who cannot attend the service. They visit the home or the convalescent hospital to provide fellowship and to diminish isolation.

HELPFUL HINTS

- Encourage and assist your parents, if they desire, to attend religious services as long as they are able. If you do not share their religious faith, arrange for them to attend, and if you do share it, join them.
- Talk with them about their spiritual concerns, and when they can no longer actively attend, encourage them to find an appropriate service on television or the radio, if they desire.
- Ask your homebound parents if they want a group from their church or synagogue to visit them. If they do, speak with those in charge and ask them to visit your parents.
- Observe the television ministry your parents follow. If the reputation of the evangelist is questionable, and you feel your parents may be taken advantage of, discuss with them the manner in which several television ministers have collected money and used it inappropriately.
- Respect their religious beliefs and help them remain connected to that which gives them spiritual well-being.

145

Spiritual Things Her World Will Allow

She had been their top volunteer. Imagine, eighty years old and doing volunteer work with the school nurse! All those wiggly, smelly, troubled kids coming in with every imaginable problem, pretended and real, to meet this skinny old lady in orthopedic shoes and a wash dress who was just right there. She called them by name, keeping their attention and holding it without ever raising her voice. They knew her name, too—a lot of people did—so when the time came that she fell and went to the hospital, her absence was noticed.

When she returned, she was slow to resume her connections. She visited school but didn't resume her regular schedule. She began to turn down rides to church. She arranged to get there on Easter and Christmas, but with significant effort, and when she didn't show, the church women put her on their list. Each week after church, a different group would visit and bring her flowers from the service. She felt embarrassed. Her son helped her with the house, but it began to look shabby. Her hair needed a wash, and the walker she was confined to made her feel ancient and unable to visit her friends.

Her son attempted to get a hairdresser to the house, but his mother refused. She had known her hairdresser for twenty-five years and was unwilling to let him see her like this. Soon she asked the women from the church not to come by. "The flowers are beautiful," she said, "but we have too many. Give them to the people in hospitals who don't have any. I saw them when I was there."

Her daughter, on a visit from California, went to the church and explained to her friends, "Look, I believe

Mother just can't face her friends seeing how crippled she has become. She is a proud and independent person. You have been important to her. She needs you, but I don't know how to handle this isolation myself."

Every so often, the minister called a few days ahead and asked if he could visit. Finally, Mother said yes; she had washed her hair and put it up the day before, a task that took all day. She was gracious and made him feel at home as she had to all the people who had come to her home over the years, but when he left she went to bed exhausted.

Her daughter said to a friend, "If my mother were not so cantankerous and independent, she'd be a fitting target for these television preachers, but, as it is, there is little in the way of a fellowship that the church offers by sitting in front of the tube. A bird and a room full of plants offer the only spiritual things her world will allow now." Because of her link with growing things and her desire to make all things as good as possible in this last difficult transition, she seemed content with it.

The best her children could do for her was to give her a bigger, more lovely cage and to find new plants, growing lights, and plant food. She never complained of loneliness Sunday after Sunday sitting alone there, but her children wondered.

Giving Up Driving

Being able to drive is a symbol of independence and competence. For an elderly parent to have that access to mobility is a treasure to family members who often boast about their parents' continuing to drive well into their nineties. However, a time will be reached when driving is dangerous to the elderly and to others and it must be discontinued. The way the situation is handled is important. Try not to make pronouncements: "You're getting too old to drive," or "I think it's dangerous to let you drive at your age." These putdowns complicate their sense of diminishing capacity. Also, losing access to driving may isolate parents and present hardships for them and other family members. Handle this change with sensitivity and, most importantly, provide alternatives that allow them to remain in touch with their surroundings and friends.

HELPFUL HINTS

- Discuss giving up driving with your parents when you detect potential problems and dangers. Encourage them to consider other means of transportation.
- Encourage parents to follow the dictates of those who test them at the motor vehicles department, especially if there are conditions, restrictions, or prohibitions.
- Arrange alternative transportation for necessary mobility: yourself, other family members, friends, local senior bus or van transportation, shared car pools, and volunteer-assisted transportation.

A Quiet Deception

Everyone knew her driving days were over. At eighty-five, she took out the left side of a parked delivery van, obliterated a crosswalk sign, broke her hip, and suffered a

148

concussion. That was her third accident in the past two years.

"My mother shouldn't drive anymore, but she won't give up," the daughter told a friend. "Even though she's been in pain and her immaculate Dodge Valiant is totaled, she's determined to get a new car. I don't know what we'll do."

While Ruth was in the convalescent home after having been let go by the hospital, she never mentioned the accident. Ruth dutifully used her walker to drag herself down the old linoleumed hall, keeping her eyes down. She couldn't bear to see two fellow inmates restrained and crying out in the night. She put wet Kleenex in her ears at night to bar their pathetic sounds. Ruth knew she'd get well and get out. She did.

Six months later, after a hip replacement, new glasses, and care at home, Ruth declared she was ready to drive once more.

"The insurance from my big Dodge should cover the costs of one of those itty-bitty new cars," Ruth told her children. This statement marked the unhinging of the intimacy that had grown over the years between mother and daughter—an intimacy that allowed for white hot disagreements to be forgotten in five minutes. This time, their eyes would not meet. The daughter did what she said she'd never do: She manipulated her mother.

"Okay, Mother, Saturday after next we will go and look at cars, but on only one condition: The purchase must be approved by an accountant."

Her mother agreed.

Once a week they spent an afternoon at a car dealership.

Ruth was exhausted, befuddled by the prices, warranties, options, colors, and equipment.

"I can't remember all this stuff," Ruth complained after many sojourns to the car dealers. "You do it for me," she said to her daughter, who now realized the delaying tactics were working.

The hunt was resumed.

Another two months went by—more time for her mother to heal and to become accustomed to being without a car.

Finally, Ruth inquired, "Aren't you ever going to get me a car?"

This direct question aroused guilt over the deception. A week later, Ruth was presented with a behemoth of an American-made car. "The accountant says it's a deal." Indeed it was. The car, although beautiful, had no power steering, no air-conditioning, and it proved to be hot and uncomfortable. Ruth drove it sparingly. She had become accustomed to riding to church with friends, and her daughter drove her to appointments and the shops.

"It worked," the daughter told her brother. "She doesn't want to drive anymore. She has a car and her dignity. Perhaps we won't be making those trips to the hospital anymore. Others will also be safe."

That was all she could do. Her first real deception was on the side of the angels.

It's Never too Late to Learn

From situations in which aging becomes the teacher, wittingly or not, wisdom is passed on to subsequent generations. Thus, whenever possible, encourage opportunities in which different generations connect. In some situations, an extended family shares a home, and the generational exchange is natural and consistent. Yet, many aging parents remain bereft of contact with the young and miss this stimulation. Adult children can help bring the two together and learn lessons as well.

HELPFUL HINTS

- If there are no grandchildren, assist your parents in seeking contact with other young people by finding out about senior volunteer programs that unite the generations.
- Encourage your parents to share their experiences and talents with the young. Teaching young people about old ways is a great tradition in many cultures, and it can be revived in families that have lost this art.
- Do not force your parents to participate in intergenerational activities if they prefer to be detached from the young.

Billy's Visits

He wasn't going to be a fireman. None of that policeman stuff either. At ten, Billy was what he aspired to be—a fisherman. He sat there on the sweaty front seat of the truck with a three-day dirty bare foot up on the dash talking about his last catch. This was the third or fourth time in detail: the bait, the line, the weight, the subtlety of fishing around the reeds on the shoreline versus around the piling under the dock. This triumphant catch had erased the hours of futile casting, rebaiting, and relocating among the pathetic puddles we managed to find along the road on our journey from California to Texas.

On the last stop, about 500 miles from Dallas, we had pulled into another sunbaked God-awful small Texas town for gas. Billy spied, over to the left, yet another stagnant pond in the afternoon sun. To Billy, it was a lake in the middle of a beautiful park. A lake filled with fish, and he begged for just a half hour to try his luck. My reluctant accession was accompanied by one last very pushy prayer to the Almighty that if He was going to do anything for this boy, this was the last chance, because I was through with these fruitless stops by stagnant waters and exhausted with days of pleading for one more stop in the 110° heat.

It took about twenty minutes before the message was received. Billy had changed bait for the third time when the fish struck. It was surefire intervention—no doubt of it. That half-sick little catfish struck and came up looking like a marlin off the Florida Keys. Never mind it was so polluted I wouldn't have dared bury it in my garden! It was heaven-sent, and we stopped for ice to pack it in the plastic foam chest for Grandma.

Despite repeated ice packings, five hundred miles later the catfish had undergone some changes. When I saw my mother through the door putting one foot in front of the other, bending over her walker as she shoved it forward, I knew I would be in the market that night looking for catfish for dinner.

Grandma didn't care that she was saying "hello" to five days of sweat and road dust. She didn't acknowledge that we smelled just like the sticky ice chest we had carried in. We poured cold drinks into glasses that, in the forties, came with cottage cheese. We sat at her kitchen table and went over each place we had stopped between California and Texas—all the stagnant ponds, all the manmade lakes, all the hopeless culverts, all the ones that got away. My mother listened with total attention to the names of lures, the bait Billy had purchased in Needles, the bait in Childress, the bait in Wichita Falls. He wasn't hers. I was hers. I was the one she longed for, but he was the one who needed and he was the one who got. I watched it with fascination.

Having no children of my own and having no grand-children in the family, my own childhood was over and was unexamined by the perspective another generation can bring. Mother had had three children but not one grand-child. I'm sure she thought the burden more difficult for her children than herself. I never heard her utter a single word of complaint in the matter. Not once. She had had her share of sorrows as anyone does who puts in their time, but her handling of this one made me aware of how very hard she concentrated on taking the good that life had to offer. In the hands of a lesser soul, this might have lent itself to doctrine or, worse yet, a sickening Pollyanna response to life. What it seemed to do for my mother was to make her evermore present and more open than most people her age. She was, after all, 88 years old and feeling every year of it. I was sweaty, in my fifties, watching this crippled, forgetful old woman weave her spell on her son's adopted grand-child. She ignored all the trouble he came from. She was there in his bait shops. She moved with him from shore to dock. He told it like a pro. She listened like a champ. Her *eyes shone; no evidence of the repetitive questions or debilitating memory loss I had been so disturbed to see on my last visit. Her timing was perfect. She humored and teased him, then fell solemn and nodded in the face of a huge lie. I was not only watching a four-star performance, I was watching my first years of teaching when I knew little or nothing of my subject matter, was a page ahead of my students and winging it all by the seat of my pants. All I had was perfect love and the timing that goes with it. I had always thought I was a natural. That's what my colleagues told me. I now saw I had been taught by a master.*

Billy flew back to California to meet his other set of grandparents for another commitment just two days later. That evening, my mother declared her dinner had been "awesome" and she was "beat." She slept much later in the mornings for several days. I was the youngest and only girl. In my mind, my place in her heart was undisputed. It wasn't a lack of love I saw in her eyes; it was that the boy had lit a fire and his presence kept it burning. Now that he was gone, something had gone with him. Perhaps it was just simple fatigue. He did require more than many children, but to my mind there was something more fundamental taking place. The boy had plunked his little body next to my mother's bones. He had emptied his pockets and shown her each and every one of his treasures, and she had followed him into eternal life. It wasn't too complicated, really.

Hucksters and Unwanted Intrusions

Junk mail, scams, door-to-door fraudulent sales, health quackery, and other unwarranted intrusions haunt many older Americans. Everybody is bombarded with promotional mail, unsolicited telemarketing, and personal sales pitches with the express intent to sell a product or service or to seek investments. Some are illegitimate and intend to cheat prospective consumers. Children of elderly parents should be on guard to protect against these abuses. While many promotions are acceptable and within legal grounds, some confuse the elderly because their enticement may be appealing and provocative. Some promotions give the impression that products or services are given free of charge, a miraculous cure for aging is available, or a grand prize awaits those who respond. And telemarketing fraud accounts for billions in investor losses annually.

Perhaps the most cynical of these ripoffs are made by those who promote products that claim to reverse aging and cure ailments associated with old age. Unsuspecting customers are flooded with quack remedies that have no benefit except to line the pockets of the hucksters. Formulas to restore youth or slow the aging process may actually harm the health of your aging parent. Encourage your parent to discuss these purported miraculous cures with their physician and to use caution in assessing the pitch delivered by unscrupulous promoters.

Sad stories abound across America about the unsuspecting elderly losing their savings or going into debt on unnecessary insurance policies or fraudulent scams. Out of sheer craving for contact, the elderly may fall for that free trip to Las Vegas, that grand prize car, that sure, safe investment in oil and gas drilling.

HELPFUL HINTS

- Discuss the possibility that unsolicited offers of products and services that are received by mail, in person, or through telemarketing may be fraudulent. Point out that many older people are targets of these abuses and that caution is essential.
- Ask your aging parents to share with you any unsolicited intrusion, and let them know that you receive the same offers and enticements. Each must be evaluated to determine its merit.
- Encourage your parents to avoid using health products not recommended specifically by their physician.
- Encourage them to be critical and to avoid a spontaneous positive response to these unsolicited offers, particularly those that seek investments, financial commitments, and credit card numbers for verification.
- Assure them that being embarrassed to talk about falling victim to fraud is common.
- Discourage aging parents from inviting unannounced door-to-door salespersons into the house or apartment.
- Ask if you can see insurance policies and any other

documents that require payment to determine if they are necessary, legal, and fulfill their promises.

- Discuss how some promoters offer enticements that may never be awarded and only serve to lure the unsuspecting person to purchase a product or service.
- Report any fraud to the local district attorney or the state attorney general.

We Won a Car

Ida could hardly wait for her daughter to return from the store. She had great news to share. Her older sister had called to tell her of a special letter that had just arrived.

"Mom, you look so happy—tell me why," Kay inquired, bringing the groceries into the kitchen of their large mobile home. Kay and her mother, Ida, had shared this home for eight years. When Ida could no longer live in the old Italian family home in upper New York State, they reunited in a mobile home. Ida had now reached the age of ninety, while her daughter was sixty-eight.

"Your aunt Ann just won a car! We have to go to Las Vegas to collect it."

Casting her eyes down, Kay just whispered, "No, not again."

"Yes, the letter came today, and your aunt is already packing. She wants you to take her there to get it and drive it back. She's too old to drive; besides, she can't see at night."

"Mom, there is no car. Aunt Ann believes all that junk mail. No one will give away a car without a hitch. I'll go over and look at the letter."

Ida just sat on the sofa. "Poor Ann. She had her heart set on it."

Kay went into the kitchen and, as she put away the groceries, she thought how innocent older people are when it comes to these gimmicks. They believe that a promise is a promise.

A Will Is Not Enough

With advancing age, your parents' financial situation is important, and you can help them if they desire your involvement. All too often, parents and their children do not discuss crucial legal and financial matters. With some parents being afraid of their children and others believing that everything is settled, frequently no one broaches the topic. Find out what their wishes are in these matters. They may welcome the opportunity to plan ahead with their children before a crisis hits. Pick the proper time and setting and include one or more siblings, an attorney, or a friend. Make it businesslike but warm and supportive. Siblings should agree in advance that they will follow their parents' decisions, except where there is ample reason to question them. Maintaining the parents' authority and independence is crucial.

Decisions mutually agreed to by parents and children are the best. Make sure that your parents do not get the impression you bring up these matters to discover what you may inherit. Reassure them that you want them taken care of as they age and that catastrophes can be avoided.

HELPFUL HINTS

- Ask your parents to list their assets (bank accounts, insurance policies, certificates of deposit, and others). Place the list in an envelope and put it in a safe place. You can now be aware of their financial resources when the need arises.
- Learn what their immediate regular income is: social security, pensions, employment. Is this income sufficient?
- Review insurance policies to find out if coverage is adequate and/or overlapping and unnecessarily duplicative.
- Suggest that your parents appoint a durable power of attorney in addition to the durable power of attorney for health care decisions. They may become incapacitated and need someone they trust to manage their financial concerns.
- Consider having them replace their will with a living trust. The single most important reason to have a living trust is to avoid the expense in time and money on probate. With a will, the estate does not go directly to the heirs but must pass through probate. Have your parents learn about the workings of a living trust from their lawyer or the county bar association.
- Learn where your parents keep their important documents (safe deposit boxes or home safes), who has access to them, and how they can be accessed in case of an emergency. Your parents' plans will not work if you do not know about them.

Record the Past

Our elderly parents have lived during the most rapidly changing times mankind has ever experienced. This is a century of social, economical, political, moral, and scientific upheavals. When they die, a large part of our most colorful history will pass with them if we fail to record their remembrances of early days. With the availability of cassette tape recorders and video cameras, oral history is easy and exciting to record. In addition to supplying the family with a personal record of their heritage, the project may increase the sense of importance of an elderly parent.

HELPFUL HINTS
- Ask permission of your parents to prepare an oral history. If the project is agreed to, plan its execution.
- Obtain the proper working equipment (cassette recorder and/or video camera) and learn how to use them. Teach your parents how to operate them, if they do not already know.
- Select a mutually agreeable setting and time and proceed with the project. You may want to ask questions in an interview format to encourage your parents to respond.
- Address any apprehension by telling your parents that a natural, conversational response is the best one—just talk.

- Make copies for other family members and relatives who wish to maintain their family record. Keep the tapes in a safe place for future generations to enjoy.

A Little Oasis of Freedom

On the farm, we had a beautiful life. My father owned it. The town was small and, like all the towns in the South, it was segregated. We were in the midst of segregation but we had a little oasis of freedom. We didn't have the usual situation of having to work for white people. Louise asked me today, "When did you learn to curse?" and I said I learned it from the field hands. We didn't have it around the house, but I thought if I'd have to be a man, I'd have to learn to curse.

There was one day I'll never forget. The authorities seemed to give my father as much esteem as was possible then between blacks and whites. I'll never forget the day the chief of police—I was deathly afraid of the law, and one day we were in town. The chief came up to the wagon and said something. Just seeing him scared me, and tears commenced to fill my eyes. My father turned to me, "Oh, Gerard, he's all right." And he took my hand. The chief looked at me and said, "Boy, if all the people was like your father, I wouldn't have no job."

When my father left Bamburg, they gave him a letter of recommendation signed by all of the officials, the merchants, the banker, the newspaper. They gave him a recommendation—"To whom it may concern." He used it to get a job in Tampa.

No Soap

"Look ahear," I said, "No soap! Pluck chickens, slaughter pigs, clean house with no soap. Impossible. I can't make soap with four little ones underfoot. That lye—that lye will eat right through fat, bones, and children's eyes."

I had lived long enough in the country to see and hear about hideous accidents caused by lye. So once a year I sent the children to Grandma's or to a neighbor for the day. I told my husband as he left with the children, "Tell Grandma there'll be extra soap from this batch."

The earth smelled warm and the constant woodfires of winter were silent. The stove was cleaned, and the ashes were shoveled into the hopper awaiting water to be poured over them in order to collect the lye. Fat and bones collected all winter sat in the huge soap barrel in the front yard by the long porch. A jar caught the lye as the water ran through the ashes into a funnel below the hopper. I relayed the lye-filled jars back and forth to the fat-filled cooking pot. By nightfall, the soap must be ready. I knew that making soap in the dark was dangerous.

I wasn't a cautious person; prudent perhaps. Girls from the prairie were often named Prudence for good reason. When the children were old enough, they could remain to help make soap.

The iron pot hung over an open fire in the front yard. Black women washed white people's laundry in cauldrons like this one, usually in their front yards over wood fires. I watched and stirred the coarse, foaming mixture.

As I watched the family truck wind down the long

*driveway, I noticed someone riding in the front seat with
her husband. It was my cousin Constance.*

*"Good to see you, Constance. This will be a day of
cooking and talking."*

"Glad to help out, Cousin Virginia."

*Four children and a husband, hard work, and life on
the prairie didn't leave time for loneliness, but loneliness
didn't need much space to take hold. The town, church,
and neighbors were far away. Having help from another
woman in mid-week was a treat. I was accustomed to
telling my friends that lonesomeness in the country had a
sound to it. It was like a ringing in the ears, with a pitch so
high that only dogs and lonely people could hear.*

*Today, with soap to make and a cousin's help, the
ringing would disappear.*

The Painted Lady

*Grandma Thomas and I had spent the morning clean-
ing the parlor for the meeting. We had dusted the large,
square player piano, the parlor lamp, the mirror that hung
above the mantle, and the straightback chairs neatly posi-
tioned for the ladies of the WCTU (Women's Christian
Temperance Union). The pictures that hung over the
wildflower wallpaper were mostly framed photographs of
family members. A log fire crackled in the grate, serving to
warm the room with a high ceiling and large windows half
covered by tan shades. The three cornered cupboards held
the dainty porcelain cups and saucers that we would use to
serve warm homemade cider to our guests.*

*Grandmother Thomas was to receive an award, a gold
broach—she was the oldest member of the McKenzie*

WCTU chapter, and her friends would gather that afternoon to honor her work to gain prohibition of spirit beverages for the nation. I, one of the youngest members, would see to it that the occasion was fitting.

After dusting and polishing the brass ornaments, we shook the flowered rugs and ran a damp cloth over the Empire couch that was covered with green mohair upholstery. Finally, we took the large volumes from the bookcase and dusted each one.

"When you finish making the refreshments, I'm going to make you pretty," I told my grandmother.

"With what?" she inquired.

"Oh, I got some things at the store yesterday. You'll see." While I was away for college, I learned about cosmetics and beauty aids. Grandmother Thomas would surprise them with her modern look; she was seventy-four years old, and the year was 1912.

The final cleaning task was to rub oil on the heavy oak door and mantle. Grandmother Thomas went to the kitchen to fix the popcorn balls. She was close with her money and decided to make something easy and simple. Popcorn rolled in molasses and served with hot cider was just the thing, she thought.

"Are you ready to get beautiful?" I sat by the older woman, near the large window in her bedroom. I lighted the oil in the curling iron lamp to heat the curlers and took strands of long gray hair and wrapped them around the warm curling iron and held each section until the curl took. When the curling was completed, I ran a comb through the tight curls and saw my grandmother's first waves cascade to her shoulders. No one had ever curled her hair before.

Next I took the two jars of cosmetics paint, one red and

the other black. I dipped the brush in the black paint and applied it to the eyebrows. I put the red rouge on each cheek and spread it softly across the cheekbones. Finally, I painted each lip with red liquid and asked my grandmother to assess the beauty conversion in her mirror.

"I've never looked like this before. I like it. Did you learn all this at college?" Grandmother Thomas turned her head from side to side.

"You look beautiful. Let's get you dressed now. They'll be here soon." Grandmother Thomas dressed and stood by the mirror for a long time, admiring the unfamiliar reflection.

"I'm dressed up for the first time in my life," she whispered.

As the women filed into the parlor, they noticed the makeup and the curls and no one said a word. Whether they were speechless or respectful, they noticed but made no comment.

While the meeting's business was being concluded, Aunt Minnie arrived from the one-room school where she taught the small town's children. Upon seeing Grandmother Thomas, she gasped and glared at me. "How could you do this?" she whispered between clenched teeth.

After the chapter's president, Mrs. Moore, pinned the broach and congratulated the recipient for her long struggle with those who let demon rum prevail, Grandmother Thomas and I served the warm cider and popcorn balls. As I watched the older women with dentures struggle with the sticky syrup and hard popcorn, trying to maintain their composure as well as their upper plates, I smiled and wondered if my grandmother had some devilishness in her also. *"I got it from somewhere,"* I later said to my grand-mother.

When the guests departed, Aunt Minnie took no time before she launched her verbal attack on me for painting the old woman with all that color and curling her hair like a floozie.

"Minnie, calm down. Inez made me feel good today. Leave her alone."

Come Up a Cloud

I watched the dark clouds gather on the horizon. In the flatlands of west Texas, you could see a long way. The wind was beginning to stir as I picked the clothes from the barbed wire fence I used to dry the clothes on. Tagging along with me, the four-year-old watched the tumbleweed roll across the yard and ran to catch a small one.

"Son, we'd better get inside. It's coming up a cloud," I called out as I gathered the last small garments from the wire.

We hurried to the porch, and I gave one last look at the storm. They moved fast across the plains, and this one looked bad. It felt bad. I was glad my other three children were at school. I knew they'd be safe there. The wind was blowing like fury.

"Mama, are we gonna use it?"

"Yes, son." I lifted the door in the floor that led to the storm cellar. Of all the houses we'd lived in, and there were a bunch during the 1920s, none had a storm cellar. I credited this providence to my prayers. This one would be a bad one. I could tell. We climbed down the wooden steps

into a cool earthen cellar beneath the house. The rich smell of red clay dirt gave us a good feeling.

"I like it down here. Can I play down here, Mama?"

"We'll see." I sat on the earthen ledge and gathered my son in my arms. I held him tightly and could not push out the memory of another son who had died the year before. Flux took him. I remembered how he suffered when the blood rushed from his bowels and nothing could stop the diarrhea. Doctors were hard to come by in places we lived. My arms were hurting the young boy, but he did not cry out.

"I hope the cow doesn't get hit by anything. She'll get to cover."

"When can I learn to milk her?" Talking kept his mind off the storm. We heard the beams crack and groan in the wind.

"You'll be old enough soon. I'll teach you then." I always made sure the family had one thing—a cow. All my life, I'd milked. "I'm not going to teach Bernice," I whispered to myself. "If I don't teach her, she'll never have to milk like I have."

I wanted my daughter to grow up to do other things. Never mind, I thought, there's a ton of chores out here. She'll do her share. But no milking for Bernice, my only daughter.

We sat quietly and daydreamed. When I could no longer hear the winds howl and the rain beating on the tin roof, I knew we were safe.

"The Lord answered our prayers, son." I smiled as we moved toward the stairs. We climbed together.

WHEN PARENTS AGE

"You'd never know we had one," I called out as I looked out the window to see the bright sunlight.

Storms came in fast and left the same way. I liked the storm cellar but knew we'd be moving one day, and maybe the next house would offer no underground sanctuary. That would be all right. I'd never had one before. I'd make do.

CHAPTER 5

Resources

The following resources, listed by category of need, are generally available to the elderly at the local, state, and/or national levels. Each service is briefly described, and address and telephone number are provided, wherever possible. Otherwise, the reader is referred to an umbrella city or county Area Agency on Aging for comprehensive information. A multitude of services is available, often free of charge. Use this resource section as a guide for networking in your community. The various groups usually know about each other and can direct you to the proper service. As the population ages, more resources will be available to adult children who want to assist their parents, regardless of the living arrangement.

169

Enrichments

Craft Shops and Fairs

Craft shops that sell articles made by seniors are operated in some communities. If your parent enjoys arts and craft activities and wishes to display and/or sell their products, find out if a craft shop featuring articles made by seniors is available. In addition, arts and craft fairs are operated for the same purpose.

Contact your senior citizen center or Area Agency on Aging to find these resources and assist your parents' participation.

Elder Day Care

Day care programs provide social activities and supervision for the slightly impaired and isolated elderly who are encouraged to attend the program from one to five days a week. Some centers provide health assessment, physical, occupational, and speech therapy, as well as bathing. Some churches and Jewish community centers have developed one- or two-day activity programs for the frail elderly. These programs offer a day outside their residence where they meet others in a protected setting. For children who care for their aging parents, a much-needed respite is offered. Adult education and local trips may also be available through these elder day care facilities. Some facilities specialize in services to persons with Alzheimer's disease. Transportation may be available. A fee may be charged, but many are free.

Contact the Area Agency on Aging for details.

Employment for Older Workers
Throughout the country, various older worker programs are available. If you want information in your area, contact the Area Agency on Aging or Private Industry Council.

Friendly Visitor and Telephone Reassurance Programs
Regular visits by matched volunteers can be arranged to lessen the isolation many elderly people feel. Friendships can develop with visitors of common interests. Some agencies provide daily telephone contact to elderly persons living alone and worried about their health or safety. A specific time is agreed to for the telephone calls, and, if no one answers, family and friends are contacted. These services help seniors feel involved and safe.

Contact the Area Agency on Aging or your church or synagogue to find out about these services.

Intergenerational Programs
An exciting volunteer program, usually operated under the auspices of senior citizens organizations or parks and recreation programs, bring older Americans together with young school children. This intergenerational program cultivates mutual understanding between the young and the old. It usually allows seniors to share life

171

experiences, crafts or other skills, and personal memo-rabilia. It also encourages sharing the hopes and needs of the two generations. More than tutors, the elderly become friends to their young charges. These programs usually take persons over sixty years of age who can volunteer one hour per week at a local elementary school.

Contact your local Area Agency on Aging for details.

Reading and Visual Loss

The Library of Congress works in conjunction with the Braille and Talking Books Library (BTBL) to provide equipment and books, free of charge, to eligible read-ers. Fill out an application that can be obtained from your local library and send it to the state library. The address is on the application. The application must be signed by a certifying authority attesting that the appli-cant is unable to read or unable to use standard printed material as a result of physical limitations. Competent authorities are health care providers (physician, optom-etrist, etc.)

The Talking Books collection offers a variety of good reading such as Shakespeare's plays, mystery stories, novels, and magazines. The books and special audio equipment are loaned at no charge, and no postage is required.

Contact your local public library for details and in-structions.

Retired Senior Volunteer Program (RSVP)

A program of ACTION, the Retired Senior Volunteer Program matches men and women aged sixty and over with nonprofit community organizations that need volunteer help. RSVP offers a wide variety of volunteer assignments, including opportunities for retired professionals. Through volunteer activities, purpose and community involvement are added to the daily routine of older Americans.

Contact the county Area Agency on Aging for details.

Senior Citizen Centers

Most communities have senior centers, and more will be developed as the number of older Americans grows. These centers are operated or funded by various groups: parks and recreation departments, United Way, and religious groups. Varying in size, scope, staffing, and activities, these programs offer more diverse enrichment than any other single program, both in health and social activities. Some provide tours, local day trips, games, adult education classes, physical fitness, and other health promotion programs, intergenerational activities, and senior advocacy. They encourage socialization among the participants as well as senior involvement in a variety of activities. A dynamic, comprehensive senior center is an asset to the community's elderly and their families. Contact the city offices or the Area Agency on Aging to find out about the senior center in your parents' community. Visit it with your parents, if they agree. Some provide transportation and meeting rooms for special events.

Share-A-Pet

Some communities run a volunteer program that recruits families and individuals who, with their companion animals, visit convalescent hospitals. The primary goal is to reach patients isolated through loneliness and/or illness. While a patient may no longer reach out to other people, he may respond to animals. If your parent is in medical confinement and you are miles apart, you may want to use this volunteer service.

Call the county volunteer center for details.

Shopping Assistance

Shopping assistance for elderly shut-ins and disabled persons is provided by some community agencies. The program may be run under the auspices of Catholic Charities, the local parks and recreation program, or another group that serves the needs of the aging. A volunteer takes the senior shopping for groceries, clothing, or other items and provides transportation, companionship, and/or guidance. This service is popular with elderly people who are isolated and home-bound.

Contact your Area Agency on Aging for details.

Transportation

One of the most serious problems for older Americans is obtaining adequate, reliable transportation. Most no longer drive and depend on others to help them shop, keep appointments, and enjoy recreational activities. When you are unable to assist your aging parents with their transportation needs, find other resources. Dial-a-ride, van services, and special transportation are available in many communities. A small fee may be charged.

Contact your Area Agency on Aging or a senior citizen

center to learn about transportation programs in your neighborhood.

Women in the Middle (WIM)

This grass roots group was started by caregivers in Alabama. Its mission is to raise the quality of in-home care which is presently being given, offer information concerning available resources and new procedures, provide an atmosphere where caregivers are free to ventilate and share frustrations, include those who are homebound via a telephone network and monthly newsletter, search for new resources to give even more substantial assistance in the future, and achieve these goals at no cost to the caregiver or their care receiver. WIM has produced a video tape, "Starting a Support Group for Caregivers of the Frail Elderly" (Cost: $20.00 plus $3.00 for shipping).

For free information about this grass roots group, send a stamped, self-addressed envelope to:

Women in the Middle, Inc.
P.O. Box 2811
Gadsden, AL 35903

Health Resources

Alzheimer's Disease Programs

The Alzheimer's Disease and Related Disorders Association is a privately funded national voluntary health organization with more than 1000 support groups and 160 chapters and affiliates nationwide. The program supports research, provides education and public awareness, encourages family support networks, and provides patient and family services to help present and future victims and caregivers.

A nationwide 24-hour information and referral line links families who need assistance with nearby chapters and affiliates. Those interested should call 1-800-621-0379 (Illinois residents call 1-800-572-6037). The telephone number for the national office in Chicago is 312-853-3060.

American Association for Retired Persons (AARP)

Coping and Caring: Living with Alzheimer's Disease is a booklet prepared by AARP for those who care for Alzheimer patients and others who want to learn more about the disease.

A copy may be obtained by writing to:

> AARP Fulfillment
> 1909 K Street, N.W.
> Washington, DC 20049

County Mental Health Association

Most counties operate a geriatric mental health program that offers a variety of services to the elderly and/or the children caring for them. Some provide free pamphlets addressed to grown children of aging parents. Many of these services use sliding scale fees.

If you need help in assessing the problems of your aging parents, call the county Mental Health Association.

Health Insurance Counseling and Advocacy Program (HICAP)

In addition to reading about Medicare and other insurance, most county offices on aging administer a program entitled HICAP. This program provides free information and assistance to seniors who have questions regarding Medicare, comparison of supplemental health insurance policies, claims, billing, and long-term care insurance. If your parent is homebound, home visits to explain the program and answer questions can be arranged with a counselor. No insurance is sold or endorsed. The program is needed because:

- filing Medicare or supplemental insurance claims can be complicated;
- mistakes are made by Medicare and insurance companies in processing claims;
- advertisements for insurance can be misleading or confusing;
- knowing your rights as a health consumer is important.

Consult your Area Agency on Aging for details.

Hearing Impairment

As parents age, certainly when they pass the seventy-five-year mark, hearing loss becomes a common disorder. They will need your support and understanding. For information about communications disorders, including deafness and the role of speech and hearing professionals in rehabilitation, as well as information about local direct services, contact:

> American Speech-Language-Hearing Association
> 10801 Rockville Pike
> Rockville, Maryland 20852
> 301-897-5700

Or call the Consumer Helpline:

> American Speech-Language-Hearing Association
> 1-800-638-8255

In Maryland, the number is 301-897-8682

For information in all areas related to hearing loss and deafness, including education, communication with persons with hearing loss and assistive devices (hearing aids), contact:

> National Information Center On Deafness
> Gallaudet University
> 800 Florida Avenue, N.E.
> Washington, DC 20002
> 1-202-651-5051

Home Health Service

Public or private home health services licensed for Medicare and Medicaid provide skilled nursing and other services such as physical, occupational, and speech therapies. These services are provided on a visiting basis to homebound patients. All personnel must be licensed and supervised by medical specialists. Ask your parents' physician about these and learn about their eligibility requirements. Different agencies have different rates; some have sliding scales. Some private health insurance policies pay for these services.

Contact your Area Agency on Aging for details.

Hospice

The terminally ill can spend their final days in a facility that offers a wide range of medical services. Most hospices are private volunteer organizations staffed by professionals; many charge no fee.

Contact your Area Agency on Aging for details.

Hospital Geriatrics Programs/University-based Medical Clinics and Services.

Many major hospitals, especially those affiliated with medical schools, offer specialized home-care services for the chronically ill who are homebound, as well as special geriatrics programs. Elderly patients can receive nursing care, rehabilitation therapy, intravenous therapy, and assistance in obtaining a variety of community services, such as transportation, hot meals, counseling, and others.

Call the nearest major hospital or medical school to inquire about the program and its services. In most cases, a fee is charged for services provided.

Impotence

Impotents Anonymous (IA) is available to help impotent men. I-Anon provides assistance to their partners. These self-help groups offer books and brochures. Self-help chapters are located throughout the United States. For information, send a self-addressed, stamped business-size envelope plus $1.00 for handling to:

> IA and I-ANON
> Box 5299
> Maryville, Tennessee 37802

Living Wills and Durable Power of Attorney
To obtain essential information and forms, write to:

> Society for the Right to Die
> 250 West 57th Street
> New York, NY 10107

The Society also provides a sample Living Will for your guidance. As an alternative, you may want to ask your parents' attorney or write to the state Office on Aging. Having the forms simplifies the process. In some areas, you may be able to obtain the forms and kits at a local stationery store. They have easy-to-follow instructions.

Meals On Wheels
In large communities, warm meals are delivered to homebound needy citizens. Most participants are elderly, and Meals On Wheels may be their only source of food. While the drivers are often volunteers, some groups pay professional drivers to deliver the warm meal. The program is primarily intended for low-income people, but some agencies do provide it to all who need it. Various groups have a contract for this service.

For details, call your local Area Agency on Aging.

Medicare and Supplemental Health Insurance

Learning about Medicare is important for both those who are sixty-five years and older and those whose parents are in that age group. Keep abreast of the frequently changing rules and regulations and consider ordering and studying the following free publications:

> *The Medicare Handbook—1990*
> This book provides information on:
> —Medicare benefits;
> —participating physicians and suppliers;
> —health insurance to supplement Medicare;
> —limits to Medicare coverage.

In addition, you should obtain the following free publications:

Guide to Health Insurance for People with Medicare (512)W
Discusses what Medicare pays and does not pay, types of private health insurance to supplement Medicare, and hints on shopping for private health insurance. (HCFA-02110)
Note: Free copies of this publication are limited.

Hospice Benefits Under Medicare (513W)
Describes the scope of medical and support services available to Medicare beneficiaries with terminal illnesses. (HCFA-02154)

Medicare and Prepayment Plans (515S)
Describes the health services available to beneficiaries from Medicare-certified HMOs and CMPs.
(HCFA-02143)

Getting a Second Opinion (545W)
Explains the importance of getting a second opinion for nonemergency surgery, Medicare coverage of costs, and gives a toll-free number for locating specialists in your area. (HCFA-02114)

Medicare and Employer Health Plans (602V)
Explains the law which requires employers to offer employees age 65 and older the same health insurance they offer their younger employees. (HCFA-02150)

Medicare Coverage of Kidney Dialysis and Kidney Transplant Services: A Supplement to Your Medicare Handbook (603V)
Describes Medicare benefits for people with chronic kidney disease. (HCFA-10128).

To order a copy of one or more of these free publications, write to:

Consumer Information Center
Department 59
Pueblo, CO 81009

Memory Loss

A leaflet called *10 Simple Ways to Improve Your Memory* is available by sending a self-addressed, stamped envelope to:

> Memory Assessment Clinic
> 8311 Wisconsin Avenue
> Bethesda, MD 20814

A videotape is also available from the clinic.

Other Nutrition Programs

Nutrition programs for seniors are often provided by community centers and parks and recreation programs. Authorized by the Older American Act, these centers provide a nutritious meal daily to anyone sixty or older in a setting of friendly socialization. Seniors should make reservations in advance by calling the center. Some centers provide low-cost van transportation from the home to the center.

While seniors may view the program as a form of charity, try to help your parent overcome the apparent stigma and encourage them to participate for both the nutritional and social rewards.

Call your parks and recreation department or community center for program information.

Patient Self-Determination

The Patient Self-Determination Act (1990) stipulates that any health care facility participating in the Medicare program as of December 1, 1991, is required to maintain written policies and procedures regarding advance directives (Living Wills) and the Durable Power of Attorney for Health Care. The act requires that, upon admission to the hospital or nursing home or when signing up for a prepaid health care plan, adult patients must be informed of their right to determine or refuse care by means of a legal document such as the Living Will or the Durable Power of Attorney.

Contact your Area Agency on Aging for details of this new legislation and its implications.

Physical Fitness

Pep Up Your Life: A Fitness Book for Seniors was produced by The Travelers companies and cosponsored by the American Association of Retired Persons and the President's Council on Physical Fitness.

According to the book, exercise is the key to attaining and monitoring the physical fitness necessary for well-being. Those over sixty are encouraged to follow the 15–30 minute program to maintain muscle coordination, strength, endurance, and flexibility. The exercises are based on levels of exertion, and the participant is guided in the use of the program.

For a copy, write to:

> "Healthy US," AARP
> 1909 K Street, N.W.
> Washington, DC 20049

Visiting Nurses Association (VNA)

The Visiting Nurses Association provides a variety of home health services, including quality total nursing care. With the expert care provided by the Visiting Nurses Association, the aging parent may be able to remain at home rather than being put in a hospital or nursing home. Comprehensive clinical nursing specialties are provided. Referrals to VNA may be made by a physician or other health care professionals, by a family member, or even by a friend of the patient.

Costs are covered by Medicare, Medicaid, health insurance, or the client.

VNA can be contacted directly by individuals; their number is available from the county medical society.

Housing Resources

The overwhelming concern of the elderly is living expenses, especially housing. Inflation has priced housing beyond the financial means of many. Increased property taxes are an additional burden on the elderly homeowner. Talk with your parents about the options they have to solve problems associated with their housing.

Care Management and Family Consultation (Eldercare)

Eldercare provides individualized assessment of the client's needs, arranges for necessary services, refers to community resources, and maintains a followup service that monitors changes in the client in order to ensure an appropriate care plan. Care management maximizes independence for frail older adults, allowing them to stay at the least restrictive level of care (often their own homes), and helps prevent premature institutionalization. Eldercare assesses the needs of the older adult, informs and educates the family about government entitlements and local resources, and empowers the family to meet the needs of the elderly. This private consultation service charges a fee.

For care management in your area, call:

National Association for Private Geriatric Case Management at 602-881-8008.

Consumer Housing Information Service for Seniors (CHISS)

In order to help your parents learn about the many options open to them as a renter or homeowner, encourage them to contact CHISS, a program operated by the American Association of Retired Persons (AARP), who provides the following information about ways to maintain or improve housing:

- issues to consider when you decide to remain in or move away from your home;
- ways to improve the livability of your home as you grow older;
- local home repair, maintenance, and weatherization programs;
- local in-home assistance and care programs;

- ways to increase income from your home or decrease the cost of living in it; and
- the location of safe, affordable, and comfortable housing if you decide to move within your county.

CHISS also provides AARP program materials that describe the advantages and disadvantages of various housing options, as well as guidelines for evaluating each option.

Contact your state or local office on aging or write to:

AARP Consumer Affairs
1909 K Street, N.W.
Washington, DC 20049

Homesharing

Many communities offer their seniors alternative housing opportunities. You may wish to ask your aging parents if they would consider sharing their home with a peer. Another possibility is intergenerational homesharing, which brings an older home provider together with a younger housemate or a younger family. With these housing arrangements, your parents can enjoy the benefits of financial, social, and personal assistance. Shared living programs match persons with common interests, needs, and preferences.

Contact the Area Agency on Aging to learn if your community has a homesharing program.

The National Shared Housing Resource Center (NSHRC) is a clearinghouse of information and technical assistance on shared housing. They operate local programs in communities through the United States. Contact: National Shared Housing Resource Center.

Nursing Home Ombudsman Program

Most Area Agencies on Aging offer an ombudsman program that works to enhance the quality of life in nursing homes and investigates problems, questions, and complaints between patients and nursing home managements. Certified volunteers provide mediation as well as information about these facilities.

Contact the Area Agency on Aging for details.

Tax Relief for Senior Home Owners

Most states, counties, and cities have tax relief programs for senior homeowners and renters. Ask your parents if they participate in a property tax relief or renter assistance program. Each program has its own eligibility requirements and filing periods. The size of the refund depends on household income.

To learn about these tax relief programs, contact the local or state tax office or the county assessor.

Legal and Financial Concerns

Many children need assistance when they begin to discuss legal, medical, and financial matters with their parents. Certainly, the first step is to meet with your parents and their attorney, if they have one. If not, you can, for a free referral, write to:

The National Academy of Elder Law Attorneys
655 North Alveraon Way, Suite 108
Tucson, Arizona 85711
602-881-4055

American Association for Retired Persons (AARP)

Legal Information. If you are helping your parents prepare for the time they may become incapacitated, you may wish to write for a free copy of:

Tomorrow's Choices: Preparing Now for Future Legal, Financial, and Health Care Decisions, AARP
1909 K Street, N.W.
Washington, DC 20049
202-872-4700

Legal Counsel for the Elderly (LCE). This service is conducted by the AARP. In some states, a telephone hotline offers free legal consultation for callers sixty or older. In addition, LCE recruits and trains lawyers to represent clients in court, often free of charge. For information, write:

Legal Counsel for the Elderly (LCE)
1909 K Street, N.W.
Washington, DC 20049

Legal and Paralegal Services. Some Area Agencies on Aging provide free legal and paralegal services and referrals for persons sixty years and older. Call for information.

Life Insurance/Health Insurance

Many free-of-charge publications that provide useful information about insurance and other financial planning are available. Encourage your parents to obtain them and jointly discuss them:

A Consumer Guide to Life Insurance (#C346)
What You Should Know About Annuities (#734)
How to Use Private Health Insurance With Medicare (#702)
What You Should Know About Health Insurance (#731)
What You Should Know About Disability Insurance (#733)
Staying Well—Your Responsibility (#1238)
IRAs: An Investment in Your Future (#356)
Financial Planning, Especially for Women (#370)
Securing Your Retirement Dollars (#315)

Write to:

> Order Fulfillment
> American Council of Life Insurance
> 1850 K Street, N.W.
> Washington, DC 20006-2284

Protection Against Health Quackery

In order to help your parents evaluate the many unsolicited promises made about health products:

- Send questions about specific products, a business-size self-addressed, stamped envelope and your concerns about the products to:

Consumer Health Research Institute
3521 Broadway
Kansas City, Missouri 64111

- If your parent suspects harm from using one of those health products, have them write to:

National Council Against Health Fraud
Victim's Redress Taskforce
Box 33008
Kansas City, Missouri 64114

Protection Against Scams Through Mail, Telemarketing or Door-to-Door Sales

Many older Americans fall prey to unscrupulous telemarketers who make fraudulent sales by high-pressure pitches, phony prize offers, or cheap merchandise. Your parents can protect themselves from these frauds. Have them check out the company with the Better Business Bureau. If they are the victim of telephone sales fraud, they can file a complaint with the local district attorney's office or the state attorney general's office.

- To remove your telephone number from most national telephone sales lists, write:

Telephone Preference Service
c/o Direct Mail Marketing Association
6 East 43rd Street
New York, NY 10017

- Order *What You Can Do About Crime* (D13655). It describes thirteen videotape and slide-tape programs available for purchase or free loan. Write:

    AARP Fulfillment (EE0114)
    1909 K Street N.W.
    Washington, DC 20049

- Contact your local postmaster or postal inspector about bogus mail-order investments and other businesses that use, advertise, or sell through the mail. Write:

    Alliance Against Fraud in Telemarketing
    815 15th Street, N.W., Suite 516
    Washington, DC 20005

Tax Assistance

When an elderly parent needs assistance with filing their income taxes and you are unable to assist or arrange for assistance, volunteers are available during the tax season to help seniors complete forms and tax refunds.

Call the Area Agency on Aging for details.